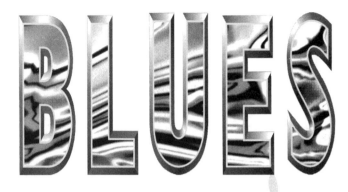

Everything about Playing BLUES

Compact Disk

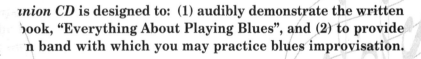

Th... ...nion CD is designed to: (1) audibly demonstrate the written
ex... ...book, "Everything About Playing Blues", and (2) to provide
you... ...n band with which you may practice blues improvisation.

STUDY EXERCISE INDEX

Table of Contents

 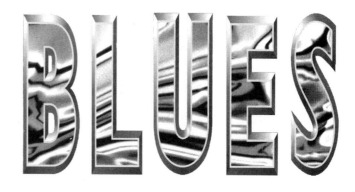

Everything about Playing **BLUES**

Section One

KNOW HOW STUFF

What is the "blues"?

Fundamentals of blues improvisation

Methods of learning blues improvisation

Blues theory

What is "Blues" Music?

Playing blues music is a way of expressing one's self. The mood may be dark, or bright and the tempo may vary from a slow melodic fell, to an upbeat hand clapping shuffle. Fast, slow, happy or sad – blues music has a story to tell. Blues music is a song with a message consisting of 12 bars of moving rhythms, riffs, and blues licks that appeal to people's moods.

Blues is about heartache, betrayal, poverty, lost love and other assorted miseries people endure as part of their everyday lives. Blues is the common language of hard-working, hard-living, hard-loving individuals that have given up on life. Pain is the binding that holdes the bluesman in bondage. He may speak of his pain and suffering; however, it is through the blues song that he is able to express his true emotions – picking the guitar, singing a sad song is *The Blues*.

The driving force in most forms of popular, improvisational music is based upon, or influenced by, the emotion and power derived from the blues scale – a simplistic five note minor pentatonic scale. Historically, certain notes considered to be out of pitch by European classical standards came to be called *'blue'* notes and were a carry over from African vocal traditions. Today, the usage of scales incorporating *'blue'* notes are the bedrock of modern blues music. These blue notes, in diatonic harmony, are the flat 3rd and flat 7th of a major scale.

Learning to play blues is gaining knowledge of what you desire to accomplish. It doesn't take a lot of talent, nor an unreasonable amount of time. What is required is the willingness to try new ideas. It does not take a prodigy to play the blues, but it does take determination and access to comprehensive information presented in a system of knowledge *that you can understand*. Of all the things required of you such as desire, determination, persistence, and open-mindedness, you must also have access to a system of knowledge. This book is that information medium. The study of the material in this book, and learning to play the examples shown are, in themselves, no guarantee of success, however the ideas expressed and the playing tips related, are essential to playing the blues.

The information contained in this book will further your music education, increase your knowledge of music, and help you to become fluent in blues music as it relates to the guitar. However, just playing notes, even solid blues riffs, will not make you a great blues musician. You must learn to use your ears.

When you are not practicing, listen to great blues players like Eric Clapton, T-Bone Walker, Robert Cray, and B.B. King. Assimilate as much of each recording as you can. Open your ears to everything being played. Listen to what the bass, keyboard, sax and drum parts are doing. Listen to how the bass player and drummer create the groove and tempo, and of course, listen to the vocals. Good blues ideas come from all of these sources and you never know what musical phrase might trigger your most compelling lick or solo.

Above all else, keep an open mind, listen to blues music, study the great blues players, and never, never give up! **WMS-RLV**

Fundamentals of Blues Improvisation

"Blues improvisation is the spontaneous creation of a rhythmic melodic line over a set group of chords called the 'Blues Chord Progression'. It involves applied knowledge and human creativity. Blues improvisation is a way of expressing oneself musically through the instrument."

–Triadic Improvisation: Wilbur M. Savidge

Musical improvisation is a language that is vibrant, fluid and inspirational. The language of music is a systematic division of the octave into 12 notes. These 12 notes lay before the guitarists' hand in marvelous fashion. Each string of the guitar is divided into the 12 notes of our musical language by the placement of the frets on the guitar fretboard.

We all have the ability to learn the language of improvisation. It is simply a matter of education, and the willingness to practice and study the art of creating music on the guitar. As with our acquired verbal skills, we must expect to invest a considerable amount of time in developing our musical ability to speak through our instrument. When we speak, we do not link words randomly. We have developed the ability to instinctively speak words that flow from our mouth without forethought. The words already exist in our mind for we have heard them used by others, and we ourselves have very often used them in patterns that correctly express our thoughts.

If this latent ability to create musical sentences that convey meaning seems to be lacking when we play the guitar, it is not that we lack cognitive skills, but it speaks of our lack of training and education. Through study and experimentation, we can become proficient in the exciting language of musical improvisation.

There is no limit to man's imagination and what he can do with the guitar. However, to play requires dedication. History has taught us that the blues musician who is best equipped with knowledge of his instrument, steeped in music theory and the history of the music he is trying to play, has the best chance to be a great blues player. Those who have developed the ability to improvise blues music have acquired the skill to capture the essence of what this style of music is all about. These guitarists have learned to extract from what others have developed and create something brand new and that the individual can call his own.

Great blues guitarists are innovators that have a firm grasp of the fundamentals of the music they play. They know their scales, chords, and melodies on a sub-conscious level. The phrases they play often are not new, but have been played before. They seem new because of the authority with which they are played.

Methods of Learning Blues Improvisation

What is the art of improvisation and how is it acquired? Is it a divine art or an inner ability with which we are born that allows the musician to effortlessly express theirself through the instrument? If not, how may we learn this magical art? Can it be absorbed from memorizing countless books on the subject, or spending hours listening to recordings of fellow musicians? How do we go about the act of spontaneously creating new and interesting music that seems to flow without thought while the fingers fret the correct notes?

Improvisation is an acquired skill much like language. It is based upon education, experience and practice. Great input is the key to the blues style.

Each blues musician borrows from his predecessors and then adds to that body of knowledge in his own unique way. Some musicians try to be creative without the benefit of listening and studying the recordings of other blues players. In this, they short change themselves, for no one achieves success solely on his own. While many blues players try to be creative without having studied other guitarist's styles, the great blues players have acquired a vast amount of historical and musical knowledge gained from reading and listening to the blues musicians that have already achieved success.

Blues improvisation is the creation of spontaneous musical expression. It is not thought about, nor planned. It is the sharing of the individual's inner world with the listener. To be successful at blues improvisation, one must apply knowledge, reasoning, feeling, intuition and sensation. You must also have a good working knowledge of harmony, scales, and the understanding of the rhythmic pulse. In essence, an improvisation is an assortment of musical ideas that are strung together to create the musical expression.

The ability to improvise may be obtained by listening to recordings, by playing with fellow guitarists, and practicing until, somehow, it becomes part of our musicianship. This is an *aural* procedure. Or, one may study books on the subject of blues improvisation, a *visual* procedure. It is through the utilization of these two mediums that one may become proficient at playing the blues.

The true essence of blues is the feelings of the player, and it cannot be expressed on the written page. But the study of written material is a valuable educational aid, especially articles in guitar magazines and guitar educational books. The shape and placement of a written note on the musical staff can by itself only indicate the note's pitch and duration. Written notation cannot indicate the *feel* required in creating blues music.

KNOW HOW STUFF

Playing the guitar is not about printed music. It is about creating sounds that are arranged in pitch, tempo, and expression to create smooth flowing solos. Printed material is a valuable educational medium and this book has been written to provide knowledge and insight on the art of playing blues. However, it can also take you beyond the page. The *Audio Illustration CD* that accompanies this book is perhaps your most valuable educational aid. Each Audio Illustration is fully demonstrated, and individual songs are played with a full back up band. The *Audio Illustration CD* has been developed so you may train your ears to interpret written examples by sound identification.

Become familiar with the placement of the notes within each scale pattern and exercise; learn the relationships between all of the notes and their sounds. Learn to play without looking at the hands so you may concentrate on the sounds that you are creating. The ability to hear changes in pitch is a vital component of spontaneous improvisation.

Each exercise, riff, and solo written in the beginning sections of this book and performed on the *Audio Illustration CD*, is played from one of the *C A G E D* system of blues scale patterns. Therefore, once you have become familiar with the finger sequence of the exercise, move beyond the printed page. Concentrate on the execution of the notes as you play and train your ears to identify the sound. Develop a set of musical and conceptual skills that let you not only see the information in print, but through practice, hear the notes in your head. If at first you find it difficult, return to the exercise and practice without the music. Train the fingers to move effortlessly without thought. Try to emulate what you hear on the CD.

Remember, blues music is about sound and its expression. Very little else really counts! As you study blues scales, you will come to realize how few notes are used to create great blues music. Simplicity is the goal!

Blues Theory

The basic tools of written musical expression are as follows: (1) **five line, four space staff** – upon which we write notes to indicate pitch; (2) **tablature** – a method of writing note placement on lines representing the guitar strings; (3) **notes** – symbols placed on the staff indicating pitch and time value (how long individual notes sustain); (4) **key signature** – which tells us the key (pitch) in which the song is written; and (5) **time signature** – which indicates what note receives one beat, and how many total beats may appear in a measure.

ILLUSTRATION ONE

THE STAFF – TABLATURE

The "staff" is comprised of five horizontal lines and four spaces. The individual lines and spaces are named for reference. The lines are: *E G B D F*. The spaces are: *F A C E*. If a pitch falls above or below the range indicated by the staff, short horizontal "ledger lines" are used.

ILLUSTRATION TWO

NOTES – RESTS

"Notes" are symbols written on the five line/four space staff to indicate a tone's pitch and duration. A written note provides two fundamental pieces of information. First, its placement on the staff indicates a fixed pitch. Second, its shape (hollow, solid, stems, flags) provides some information, though not all, as to the length of time the note must sustain in relation to the beat. Music consists of *silence* as well as sound, and each kind of note has an equivalent "rest sign". A rest sign placed on the staff indicates a note not to be played for the amount of time represented by the symbol.

ILLUSTRATION THREE

KEY SIGNATURE

The "key signature", consisting of sharp or flat signs immediately following the clef sign at the beginning of the staff, is a musical device that establishes the key (pitch) in which a composition is to be played. Each note indicated by a sharp or flat in the key signature is played sharp or flat in that key's scale. (The key of *C* does not have sharps or flats and is called the "natural key" – the key of *A* has three sharps).

ILLUSTRATION FOUR

TIME SIGNATURE – BAR LINES – MEASURES

In written form, the "time signature" is a grouping of separate numbers with one placed on top of the other, in the style of a mathematical fraction, without a line placed between them. The two numbers tell the musician how the music must be counted, and how many beats there are in each measure. The *top number* represents the number of beats in each measure. The *lower number* denotes which type of note (whole, half, quarter, etc.) receives *one count* (one beat). (*Example:* 4/4 says four beats per measure and quarter note receiving one beat. 6/8 says six beats per measure and the eighth note gets one beat.)

Vertical lines, called "barr" lines, are placed at regular intervals and divide the staff into sections called "measures" (also called bars). Each measure contains the same number of beats. The end of a song, or sections within a song, are marked by two adjacent vertical lines called a "double barr" line.

THE STAFF-NOTES-KEY SIGNATURE

ILLUSTRATION ONE
THE STAFF – TABLATURE

STAFF LINES AND SPACES   LEDGER LINES

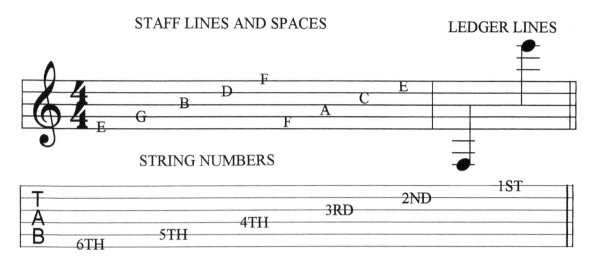

STRING NUMBERS

ILLUSTRATION TWO
NOTES & RESTS

DURATION OF WRITTEN NOTES (How long they sustain)   REST SIGNS

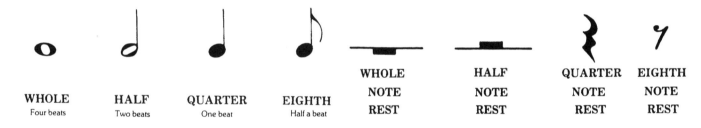

WHOLE	HALF	QUARTER	EIGHTH	WHOLE NOTE REST	HALF NOTE REST	QUARTER NOTE REST	EIGHTH NOTE REST
Four beats	Two beats	One beat	Half a beat				

ILLUSTRATION THREE
KEY SIGNATURE

SHARP KEYS   FLAT KEYS

ILLUSTRATION FOUR
TIME SIGNATURE-BAR LINES-MEASURES

Counting Time

ILLUSTRATION ONE

TIME

When playing rhythm, it is important to have some means of accurately measuring various rhythmic pulses – or "keeping time" – or knowing where you are in a measure. In blues, the most commonly used meter (beat pattern), falls in groups of four beats to a measure. This grouping is referred to as 4/4 time (also called "common time"). In 4/4 time, we count: **one**, *two, three, four,* **one**, *two, three, four,* etc. Timing is a developed skill that improves the more you play. It is the ability to play a piece without speeding up or slowing down. It involves the ability to keep a constant and even rhythm beat, and emphasizes certain notes at precisely the same moment as other musicians in the band. Tapping the foot at a steady and even tempo helps to interpret rhythmic pulse. Counting out loud is also a very helpful way of keeping time.

ILLUSTRATION TWO

TEMPO – RHYTHM

All music composition is a combination of *time, harmony* and *melody*; and are, of course, interdependent. Time is the horizontal effect of music. It is comprised of two components – "tempo" and "rhythm". "Tempo" is the speed (rate) of the beat. Specific tempo is measured as a number of beats per minute; and generally, one beat is represented by one *quarter note*. The speed of a song may be changed by increasing or decreasing the tempo played – playing more or less beats to the minute. Slow tempo is played at 40-66 beats per minute; moderate tempo is played at 108-120 beats per minute; fast tempo is played at 120-168 beats per minute. A metronome is a great device for establishing beats per minute.

The tempo sign shown in this illustration indicates that the song is to have a tempo of 98 beats per minute. "Tempo" states how long it will take to play a set group of notes. "Rhythm" indicates which of the notes are emphasized (accented) and which are not. Rhythm is the "way" in which a tempo is played. The rhythm produces the *feel* of the song.

ILLUSTRATION THREE

DOWN BEAT – UP BEAT

The rhythmic structure of a song is expressed in "beats". Notes are played in relation to the beat. There are two types of beat: up beat and down beat. Can you tap your foot without raising it? Of course not! In order to tap your foot, you must raise your toe from the floor. This raising of the toe is called the "up beat". Tap down – you have created the "down beat". The rhythm of a song is determined by the beat. Chords are played in relation to the beat – on beat, or off the beat. *Illustration Three* shows the proper technique of tapping the floor on the down beat. Tap your foot on the count **one**, *two, three, four,* etc. on the *down beat*. Tap at any speed (tempo) you desire. However, to maintain an even and constant beat, use a metromome!

COUNTING TIME

ILLUSTRATION ONE
COUNTING TIME

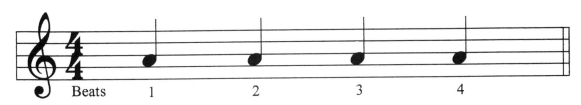

TIME SIGNATURE

MEASURE

Beats   1   2   3   4

ILLUSTRATION TWO
TEMPO ♩ = 98

Beats   1   2   3   4

ILLUSTRATION THREE
UP BEAT – DOWN BEAT

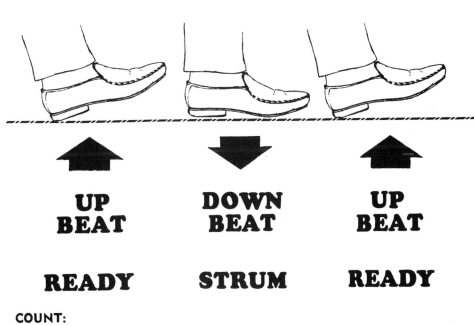

UP BEAT   **DOWN BEAT**   **UP BEAT**

READY   **STRUM**   **READY**

COUNT:

AND . . . . . **One** . . . . . AND

Applying Time Values to Tab Numbers

Before we begin our study in "riff construction", let us examine the art of applying rhythm to tablature. "Tab" numbers are *fret* numbers, the placement notes on the guitar fretboard. In most tab systems, *rhythm* is not noted. In order to accurately play tab written music, we must learn rudimentary skills in rhythm notation. We must develop our ability to read the time value of written notes. This ability does not require one to read music, but only to develop an understanding of how an individual note, or group of notes, are played in relation to the beat. The exercises on the following page will help you in developing this important aspect of reading tablature and playing the notes in proper meter.

ILLUSTRATION ONE

Illustration One, measure one, is written in quarter notes (one note on each beat). In the second measure, beat one is rested with a quarter note rest placed on the first beat and quarter notes placed on beats two, three and four.

ILLUSTRATION TWO

Illustration Two is written in eighth notes (two notes to each beat). Again, in both measures a quarter note rest is placed on the first beat.

ILLUSTRATION THREE

Illustration Three is written in triplets (three notes to each beat). The second measure begins with a quarter note rest on the first beat.

ILLUSTRATION FOUR

Illustration Four is written in a combination of notes of different time values. The first two notes (quarter notes) of the first measure are played on beats one and two. The triplet notes occur on the third beat with a quarter note placed on the fourth beat. The second measure begins with an eighth note rest which places the first note of the second measure on the up-beat between beats one and two.

APPLYING TIME VALUES TO TAB

ILLUSTRATION ONE - QUARTER NOTES

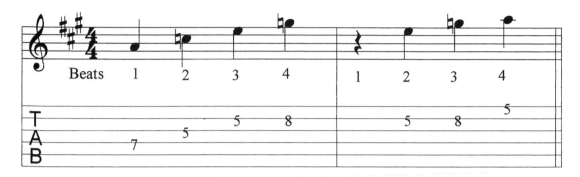

ILLUSTRATION TWO - EIGHTH NOTES

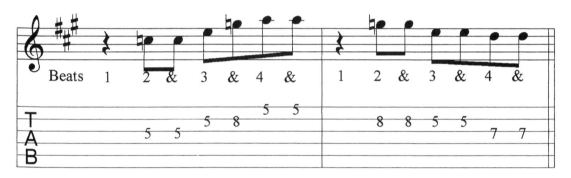

ILLUSTRATION THREE - TRIPLETS

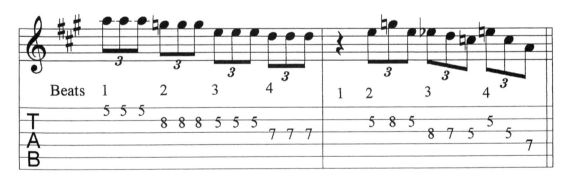

ILLUSTRATION FOUR - COMBINING NOTES

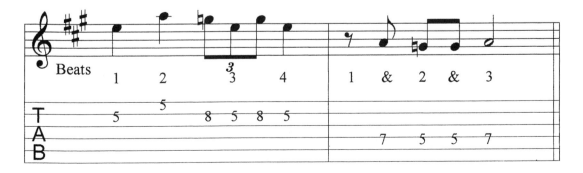

What is a Scale?

Scales are tools for developing tonality that provides the musician with a *sense of place* in the connection between tones. All music is based on the proven scientific fact that notes we use to create music have fixed rates of vibration which are mathematically related to one another. Each note has a pitch which we can produce vocally or on a musical instrument. These notes, when played in fixed patterns are called scales; and each scale produces its own unique sound.

The scale is a predetermined and logical series of notes combined within a specific pattern suitable for harmony. The scale is a structure based on the placement of tones and semitones (English terminology), or whole-steps, and half-steps (American terminology). The characteristic sound of any scale is determined by the number of tones, the order in which they occur, and by the size and placement of the interval between notes (steps and half-steps).

In our study of blues, we will explore the usage of six different types of scales: the **chromatic scale**, the **diatonic major scale**, the **major pentatonic scale**; the **minor pentatonic scale**, the **blues scale** (an altered minor pentatonic scale), and the **mixolydian scale**.

ILLUSTRATION ONE

CHROMATIC SCALE *(The Grandfather of All Scales)*. When you have two notes of the same name, but different pitch (one written higher than the other and vice versa), they are said to be an *octave* apart. All musical tones lie within the octave. Musical scales (notes arranged in a predetermined order) are established by the division of the octave into a series of ear-pleasing tones. World cultures have developed scales unlike our familiar seven-tone *do re mi* scale of Western music. However, all scales start on and return to *do*. The seven notes of the musical alphabet *A B C D E F G* are represented by the white keys on the piano; and the five accidentals, called either *sharps* or *flats*, are represented by the black keys on the piano. These notes, played in succession, descending or ascending in pitch, is a *chromatic scale*. This half-step division of the chromatic scale is accomplished on the guitar fretboard by the half-step placement of the frets.

The application of the chromatic scale in modern music is a mixed blessing. It is the grandfather scale of the parent key, for it contains all 12 notes of the key. (***Example:*** Key of *A* major. All seven notes of the diatonic *A* major scale are found within the 12 note *A* chromatic scale. Therefore, it seems to fit . . . yet, it includes five *wrong* notes!)

In our study of blues improvisation, it is important to fully understand the tonal relationship of chromatic scale notes, because it is upon the 12 note chromatic scale that we build the more simplistic five and six note scales used in blues music. The chromatic scale simply represents, in alphabetical order, our interval system of notes.

ILLUSTRATION TWO

The black and white piano keyboard presents the chromatic scale in a clear and visual way that is not as obvious on the guitar fretboard. The keys of the piano keyboard represent one chromatic scale, repeating itself in higher and higher octaves with the lowest octave on the left of the keyboard. The distance between each key, black or white, is the distance of a half-step, or the distance of one fret on the guitar.

*NOTE: For a complete, in-depth study of scales, we highly recommend the Praxis Publications book: **Everything About Scales**.*

CHROMATIC SCALES

ILLUSTRATION ONE
THE CHROMATIC SCALE

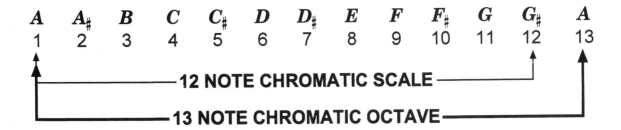

A	A♯	B	C	C♯	D	D♯	E	F	F♯	G	G♯	A
1	2	3	4	5	6	7	8	9	10	11	12	13

— 12 NOTE CHROMATIC SCALE —

— 13 NOTE CHROMATIC OCTAVE —

12 CHROMATIC SCALES

A A♯ B C C♯ D D♯ E F F♯ G G♯ A

A♯ B C C♯ D D♯ E F F♯ G G♯ A A♯

B C C♯ D D♯ E F F♯ G G♯ A A♯ B

C C♯ D D♯ E F F♯ G G♯ A A♯ B C

C♯ D D♯ E F F♯ G G♯ A A♯ B C C♯

D D♯ E F F♯ G G♯ A A♯ B C C♯ D

D♯ E F F♯ G G♯ A A♯ B C C♯ D D♯

E F F♯ G G♯ A A♯ B C C♯ D D♯ E

F F♯ G G♯ A A♯ B C C♯ D D♯ E F

F♯ G G♯ A A♯ B C C♯ D D♯ E F F♯

G G♯ A A♯ B C C♯ D D♯ E F F♯ G

G♯ A A♯ B C C♯ D D♯ E F F♯ G G♯

ILLUSTRATION TWO
THE PIANO KEYBOARD – A CONTINUOUS CHROMATIC SCALE

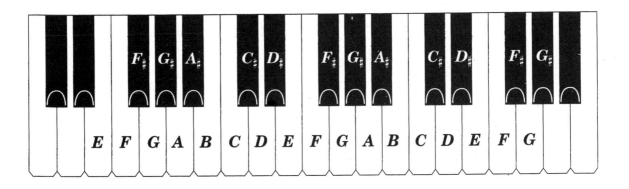

The Guitar Fretboard

The guitar is designed as a chromatic half-step instrument with the distance between each fret representing a half-step movement. The six strings of the guitar make up six chromatic scales. Each scale starts on the note in the chromatic scale upon which the guitar string is tuned and continues up the neck, ascending in pitch, until the tone is repeated again at the 12th fret. (12 fretted notes + the open string tone = one octave).

Fretboard mastery begins by understanding the note placement of each string. Acquiring this knowledge will not come overnight; however, it begins with the understanding that each of the six strings is a *chromatic scale*. Once you have memorized the names of the open strings, you have the crucial information that will allow you to determine the name of a note at any fret.

SIX CHROMATIC SCALES

THE COMPLETE GUITAR FINGERBOARD

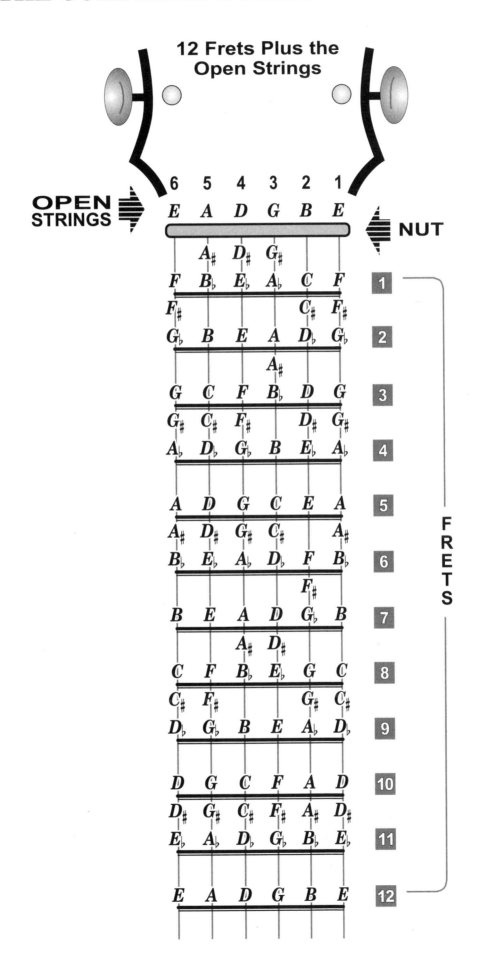

The Major Scale

ILLUSTRATION ONE

The diatonic major scale, with its familiar *do-re-mi-fa-so-la-ti-do* sound *(Illustration One)*, is the scale used to create the vast majority of the music guitarists encounter daily. It is from the diatonic major and minor scale that blues scales originate. To understand the art of blues improvisation and how blues scales are created, we must fully understand the step/half-step pattern (the degree name and number) of the diatonic scale. It is by altering the number and placement of the notes in reference to the step/half-step pattern of the diatonic scale, that blues scales are created. Chord terminology also utilizes the diatonic scale tones. Chord triads (1 3 5), and extended notes (b7 9 13), are terms that relate to the notes of the diatonic scale.

The major diatonic scale is a predetermined pattern of seven notes arranged in five whole steps and two half-steps. A half-step is the distance of one fret on the guitar. A whole step is the distance of two frets. In other words, a major diatonic scale is a succession of tones arranged in fixed whole-step/half-step patterns. The distance between notes remains constant and the intervals between notes are fixed and will not change, even if the music is played in another key. In this manner, we recognize a song and can hum the melody, regardless of the key (pitch) in which it is performed. Thus, making it possible to transpose a piece of music into other keys.

The sound of the major diatonic scale is due to the placement of whole-steps and half-steps. In the major scale, the half-steps occur between the 3rd and 4th notes, and between the 7th and 8th notes. As a result, the placement of two whole-step (step, step) intervals between the 1st and 3rd notes create the scales major (as compared to minor) tonal characteristic.

ILLUSTRATION TWO

C SCALE NOTES ON THE GUITAR FRETBOARD. Experiment with the step/half-step diatonic scale pattern on the fretboard. *Illustration Two* shows the *C* major scale. In playing the scale pattern, use four fingers. Always start the pattern with your first finger on the first note. Try other scales. Start the same pattern on the note *D*, second string, third fret. The same step/half-step pattern will produce the *D* major scale.

ILLUSTRATION THREE

C MAJOR DIATONIC SCALE – WRITTEN FORM. This illustration represents the C major scale as it appears in written and tablature form.

THE MAJOR SCALE

ILLUSTRATION ONE
C MAJOR SCALE – THEORETICAL FORM

ALPHABETICAL	C	D	E	F	G	A	B	C
ARABIC	**1**	**2**	**3**	**4**	**5**	**6**	**7**	**8**
ROMAN	I	II	III	IV	V	VI	VII	VIII
SOL-FA	DO	RE	MI	FA	SOL	LA	TI	DO
THEORETICAL	TONIC	SUPER TONIC	MEDIANT	SUB DOM	DOMINANT	SUB MEDIANT	LEADING TONE	TONIC

ILLUSTRATION TWO
C SCALE NOTES ON THE GUITAR FINGERBOARD

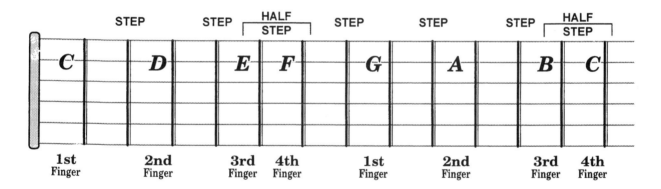

ILLUSTRATION THREE
C MAJOR DIATONIC SCALE – WRITTEN FORM

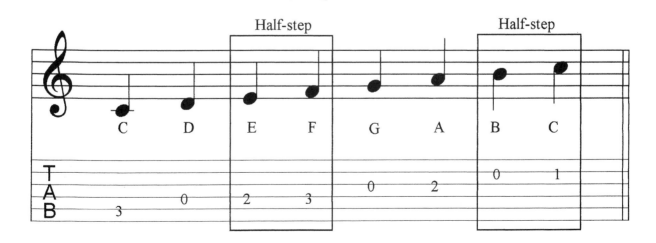

The Pentatonic Major Scale

ILLUSTRATION ONE

MAJOR DIATONIC SCALE. This scale is a major scale because of the interval between the *tonic* note (first note of the scale) and the third note of the scale. The distance between the two notes is a distance of two whole-steps. This produces a **major interval** called a *major 3rd*.

PENTATONIC SCALE. *Penta* is the Latin word for five – and a five-note scale is called a *pentatonic* scale. It is a simple modification of the seven-note major diatonic scale. A major pentatonic scale is created by eliminating the 4th and 7th notes of a major scale. The formula for a major pentatonic scale is: whole-step, whole-step, minor third, whole-step, minor third. This is a scale without half-steps. The absences of the diatonic scale's 4th and 7th notes creates a scale that is easier to utilize. With only five notes, the guitarist has less tones with which to be concerned when creating riffs.

ILLUSTRATION TWO

MAJOR PENTATONIC SCALE. *Illustration Two* is a major pentatonic scale because the distance between the first and third note is a major 3rd interval. It is a pentatonic scale, because we have deleted the 4th and 7th notes of the major scale. This illustration is a *C* major pentatonic scale.

THE PENTATONIC MAJOR SCALE

ILLUSTRATION ONE

C MAJOR SCALE

1	2	3	4	5	6	7	8
C	*C#*	*D*	*D#*	*E*	*F*	*F#*	*G*	*G#*	*A*	*A#*	*B*	*C*

STEP   STEP   HALF STEP   STEP   STEP   STEP   HALF STEP

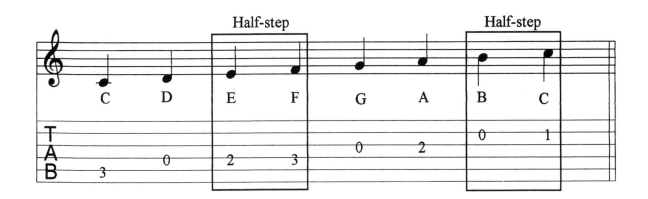

ILLUSTRATION TWO

PENTATONIC MAJOR 5 NOTE SCALE

1	2	3	4	5	6
C	*D*	*E*	*G*	*A*	*C*

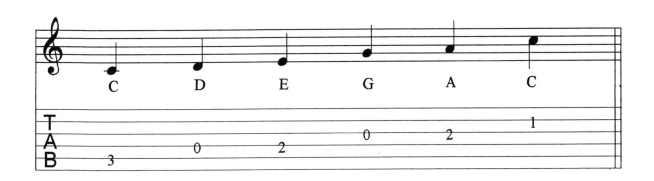

Minor Scales

The minor pentatonic scale does not possess half-steps, and may be played against the I-IV-V blues chord progression without fear of playing wrong notes! The interval structure of the minor pentatonic scale produces two distinctively bluesy notes – the flat 3rd and the flat 7th of a major scale. The application and possibilities of the minor pentatonic scale are virtually endless and it is quite popular with Country, Rock and Blues musicians. By playing minor pentatonic scales, it is possible to go outside of traditional diatonic harmony while still retaining the conventional chord harmony associated with diatonic scales.

ILLUSTRATION ONE
RELATIVE MINOR SCALE

The relative minor scale is called the natural minor and is derived from the Greek *aeolian* mode. It is a scale played from the sixth note of its parent diatonic major scale. The diatonic major scale and its relative minor scale share the same key signature and share the same notes. Because the relative minor scale starts at the sixth note of the diatonic scale, the step, step/half-step placement of this new scale contains a minor third interval which creates a minor tonality.

ILLUSTRATION TWO

ALTERED MINOR PENTATONIC "BLUES" SCALE

The minor pentatonic five-note scale is an altered relative minor aeolian scale. It is a minor scale, because the interval between the tonic and third note of the scale is a **minor third interval**. A minor pentatonic scale is created by eliminating the 2nd and 6th notes (the same notes as the 4th and 7th notes of its parent diatonic scale) of a relative minor scale. Because the scale does not contain the diatonic scale's 4th and 7th notes which provide a definite sense of direction in diatonic harmony, the blues guitarists can utilize one scale over the standard blues chord progression which is typically referred to as the I-IV-V progression.

ILLUSTRATION THREE

PENTATONIC MINOR 5-NOTE "BLUES" SCALE

Illustration Three presents the five-note "Blues" scale played in the open position.

RELATIVE MINOR SCALE

ILLUSTRATION ONE
C MAJOR SCALE

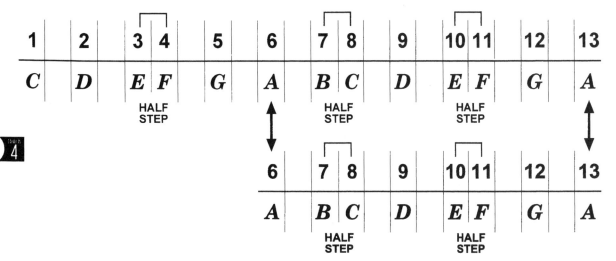

RELATIVE MINOR SCALE

ILLUSTRATION TWO

ALTERED MINOR SCALE – MINOR PENTATONIC SCALE

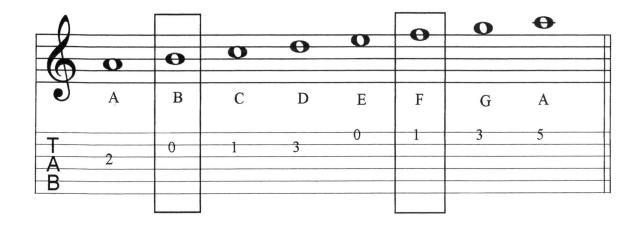

ILLUSTRATION THREE

PENTATONIC MINOR 5 NOTE "BLUES" SCALE

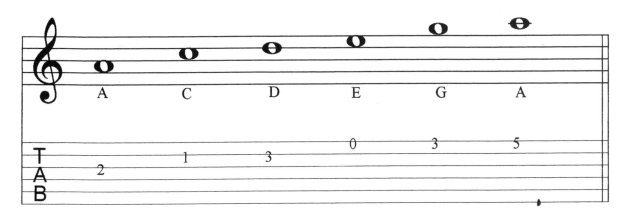

The "Blues" Scale

ILLUSTRATION ONE

The scale most often associated with traditional blues music is based upon the minor pentatonic scale (1st, flat 3rd, 4th, 5th and flat 7th). It is created by adding a raised 4th/flat 5th (#4/b5). It is the addition of this one note (we will call it b5) to the minor pentatonic scale that gives the scale the bluesy sound that has become the hallmark of modern blues music. The blues scale can be used in a variety of ways. It can be played against major chords, and like its cousin scale the minor pentatonic, it also works most effectively over minor harmony.

ILLUSTRATION TWO

MIXOLYDIAN SCALE

Blues scales come in a variety of styles, including the *mixolydian scale*. The mixolydian scale is an inversion of a major scale. This variation is called a mode when played within the parent scale. The mixolydian mode is created by playing a major scale from the fifth degree to its octave (higher or lower). When the mixolydian scale is combined with the minor pentatonic, it is commonly called the *B.B. King blues scale*.

The *A* mixolydian scale is a scale starting on the fifth note of a *D* major scale. *A* to *A* of the *D* major scale will produce the same notes as the *A* major scale played with a flat 7th or *G* natural note. It is this flat seventh (the *G* natural) that colors the scale, it is a "blue" note.

THE "BLUES" SCALE

ILLUSTRATION ONE
PENTATONIC 6 NOTE "BLUES" SCALE

1		2	3	4	5		6	7/1
A		C	D	Eb	E		G	A

PENTATONIC '6' NOTE "BLUES SCALE"

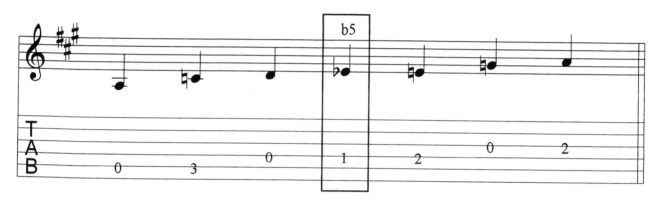

ILLUSTRATION TWO
MIXOLYDIAN SCALE

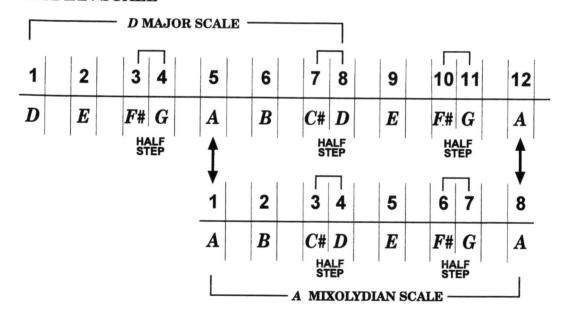

Blues Chord Progression Theory

Chords used to create the *blues groove* are uncomplicated and relatively few in number. Most blues arrangements use the basic chords every guitarist, even beginners, are familiar with. They are the major chords, such as *C* major, and dominant chords such as *C7* and extended dominant chords such as *C9* and *C13*, and minor seventh chords like *Cm7*. Complex altered and extended chords *(example: B7b5+9)* associated with Jazz arrangements are seldom used in blues rhythm patterns.

ILLUSTRATION ONE

PRIMARY CHORDS – THE I-IV-V CHORD PROGRESSION

Building diatonic triads on each note of the diatonic major scale produces the following series of chords: *I major, ii minor, iii minor, IV major, V major, vi minor, vii diminished*. Because of the *tension* and *resolution* movement of chords within keys, chords built on the 1st (tonic), 4th (sub dominant) and 5th (dominant) degrees of the scale are called the **primary chords**. The ii, iii, vi, viii chords are secondary chords. *Illustration One* is written in the key of *A* major.

ILLUSTRATION TWO

MAJOR CHORD TRIAD

The formula for a major chord triad is *R 3 5*. In chord construction, the tonic note of the chord is referred to as the root. Every interval has an effect on the sound of the chord. However, it is the root tone that determines the chord's identity. In this manner, the chord name is the same as the name of the parent scale. (*Example:* In the key of *A* major, a chord built on the first note of the scale is an *A* type chord.)

ILLUSTRATION THREE

MINOR CHORD TRIAD

The formula for a minor chord triad is *R b3 5*. It is the *b3* (1-1/2 steps) that creates the minor sound.

PRIMARY CHORDS

ILLUSTRATION ONE
THREE PRIMARY CHORDS

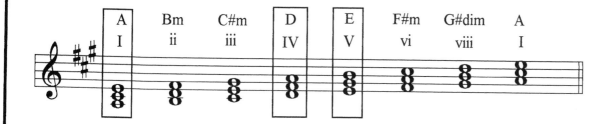

A	Bm	C#m	D	E	F#m	G#dim	A
I	ii	iii	IV	V	vi	viii	I

ILLUSTRATION TWO
MAJOR CHORD TRIAD 1 3 5
A C# E

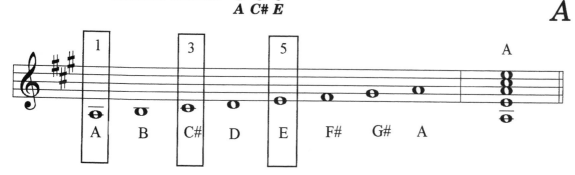

A   B   C#   D   E   F#   G#   A

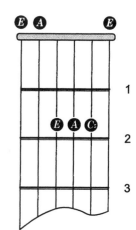

A

ILLUSTRATION THREE
MINOR CHORD TRIAD 1 b3 5
A C E

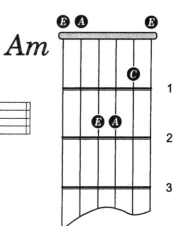

A   B   C   D   E   F#   G   A

Am

Dominant Chords

The evolution of triad harmony established the prominent role of the dominant (V) chord in chord progressions. Adding a minor third interval to the dominant triad creates a *dominant seventh* (V7). The usual abbreviation for a dominant seventh chord is simply to refer to it as the *seventh* – for example, *A7*.

ILLUSTRATION ONE
DOMINANT SEVENTH CHORD

The formula for a dominant chord triad: **R 3 5 b7**

In *Illustration One*, we show an *A7th* chord played at the fifth fret. The *root note* of the chord appears on the first and sixth string. Since there are no open tones in the chord, the chord is moveable.

EXTENDED DOMINANT CHORDS

Adding a note that is more than an octave above the root to a dominant chord will produce an *extended* chord, such as *7th, 9th* and *13th*. If the second note above the root is inverted an octave above the root, and added to a dominant chord, the new chord is called a *ninth*. If the 6th note above the root is inverted an octave above the root, and added to a chord, the new chord is called a *thirteenth*. To facilitate this additional note, it is common practice to drop the 5th of the chord. The major third must be retained for it is this note that defines the chord as a major chord.

ILLUSTRATION TWO
DOMINANT 9TH

The formula for the dominant 9th chord triad: **R 3 b7 9**

The dominant 9th chord is a popular substitute for the dominant seventh chord and is commonly used by blues musicians. In *Illustration Two*, we show an A9th chord played at the sixth fret. The *root note* of the chord, the note that determines the chord's name, appears on the fourth string. The chord is movable, its name at each fret determined by the notes of the fourth string chromatic scale. The dominant 9th chord is commonly used as a substitute chord in blues chord progresisons.

ILLUSTRATION THREE
DOMINANT 13TH

The formula for the dominant 13th chord triad: **R 3 b7 9 13**

The dominant 13th chord is a popular substitute for the dominant 7th chord and is commonly used by blues musicians.

In *Illustration Three*, we show an *A13th* chord played at the fifth fret. The root note of the chord appears on the first string.

NOTE: Not every note of the chord formula will always be present within a chord. This is acceptable and allows for easier chord fingering.

For a complete and in-depth study of chord construction, we recommend
Praxis Publications' *books:* **Everything About Chords** *and* **Everything About Scales**.

DOMINANT CHORDS

ILLUSTRATION ONE
DOMINANT SEVENTH *A7* (1 3 5 b7)
A C♯ E G

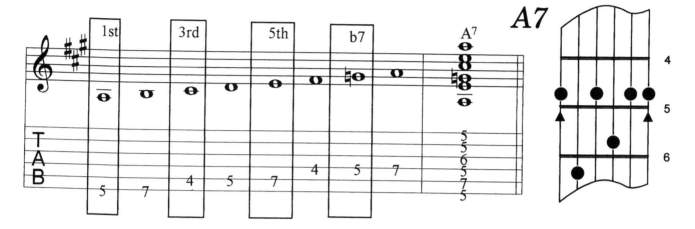

ILLUSTRATION TWO
DOMINANT NINTH *A9* (1 3 b7 9)
A C#G B

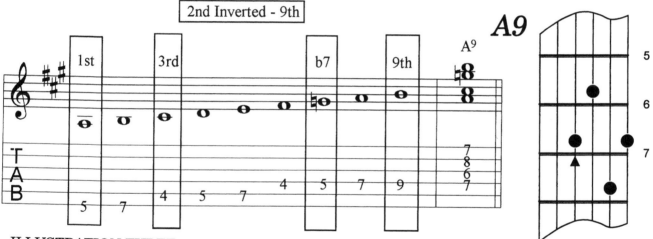

ILLUSTRATION THREE
DOMINANT THIRTEENTH *A13* (b7 3 13 1)
G C♯ F♯ A

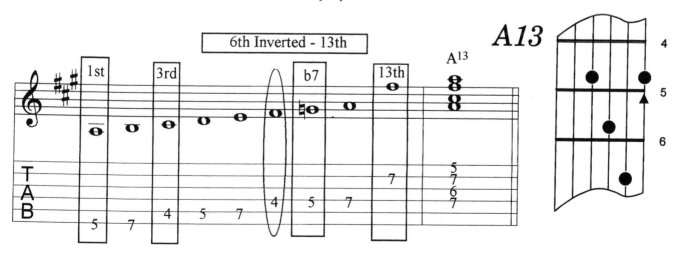

Alternate Dominant Chord Fingerings

If the lowest note in a chord is not the root, the chord is said to be *inverted*. When the root note is the lowest note, the chord is said to be in the *root* position. (Example: *A7 ROOT – A, C#, E, G*). When the lowest note is the 3rd, the triad is called the *first inversion*. (Example: *A7 THIRD – C#, E, G, A*). If the 5th of the triad is the lowest note, the chord is said to be in the *second inversion*. (Example: *A7 FIFTH – E, G, A, C#*).

The principle of triad inversion allows chords to be played on the guitar in an almost infinite variety of *voicings*. Each inversion creates a different fingering pattern. However, only a few are in common usage. On the following page, we present the more common patterns used by blues guitarists. Black triangles indicate the root note. The patterns are all moveable.

Chord Terminology

FULL CHORD

A full chord is a chord consisting of its root (1), 3rd, 5th; and if used, its extensions – 6th, 7th, 9th and 13th. A full chord may utilize from four to all six strings of the guitar.

PARTIAL CHORD

A partial chord is a chord in which individual triad tones have been eliminated. The fifth tone is often omitted when extension tones are added. A partial chord may use as few as two or three strings.

OUTSIDE CHORD

An outside chord is a partial chord utilizing the *outside* strings (the 4th, 3rd, 2nd and 1st strings). An outside chord may utilize as few as two strings.

ALTERNATE DOMINATE CHORD FINGERINGS

7th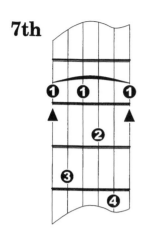

9th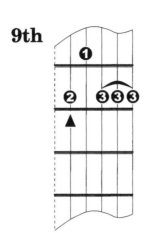

13th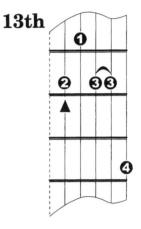

7th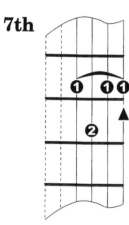

9th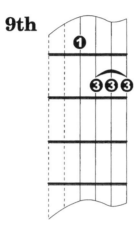

13th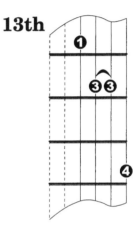

7th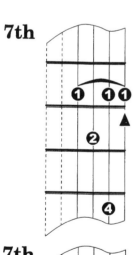

9th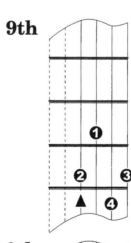

13th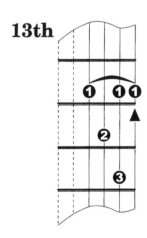

7th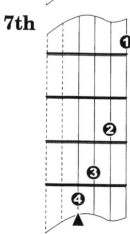

9th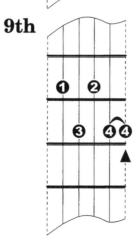

12-Bar Standard Blues Chord Progression

ILLUSTRATION ONE

The I-IV-V chord figure defines the blues chord progression. However, it does not imply the sequence in which chords appear in a blues song. It is a statement explaining the type of chords that normally occur within a 12-bar arrangement. It represents the three most important chords within a key. These chords are called the *primary chords*, or the **I-IV-V** chord set. Over the years, rules have been established to govern the movement of one chord to another (a *progression*). Their function is to organize chord changes within a key so that the tonic chord (built upon the first note if the scale) is clearly the home chord. The **IV** chord is built on the fourth note of the scale and is called the *sub-dominant chord*. The **V** chord is built on the fifth note of the scale and is called the dominant chord. These three chords will always sound good when played together and in whatever order they are placed, or in whatever key they are played.

ILLUSTRATION TWO

In the evolution of triad harmony, the *dominant chord* has developed a prominent role in the chord resolution (chordal movement). To facilitate this dominant resolution, a fourth note is added to the dominant chord triad, thus creating a four-tone chord. In blues music, the dominant chord is always played as a seventh, hence the **V** chord becomes a **V7**.

12-Bar Blues Dominant Chord Progression

Blues chord progressions have a very specific form in terms of the length (how many measures), and the type and placement of the chords (chord pattern). The most common blues progression is a set pattern of chord changes called a **12-bar progression**. It takes 12 *bars* (measures) to complete each cycle. Then, the progression is repeated as many times as one wishes to continue the song. There are several blues variations, or changes in the chord pattern. One pattern is only eight bars in length. For now, we will begin our study of blues rhythm with the basic 12-bar pattern shown in *Illustration One*.

12-BAR CHORD PROGRESSION

ILLUSTRATION ONE

12-BAR STANDARD CHORD PROGRESSION

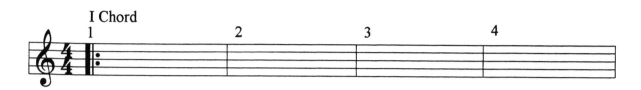

I Chord
1   2   3   4

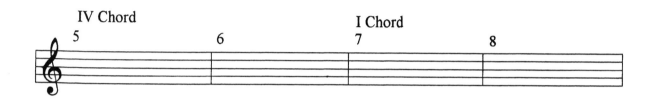

IV Chord
5   6   I Chord
7   8

V Chord   IV Chord   I Chord   V Chord
9   10   11   12

ILLUSTRATION TWO

12-BAR DOMINANT BLUES CHORD PROGRESSION

KEY OF A

A7   A7   A7   A7

D7   A7

E7   D7   A7   E7

12-BAR "QUICK-CHANGE" PROGRESSION

12-Bar "Quick-Change" Blues Chord Progression

The most common 12-bar blues chord progression makes a *quick-change* to the IV chord in measure two. The IV chord is played for one measure, then the progression moves back to the I chord for two measures before going to the IV chord in measure five.

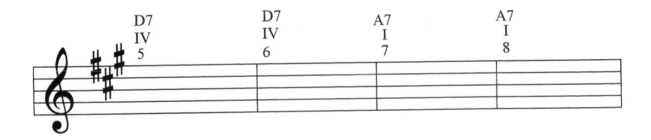

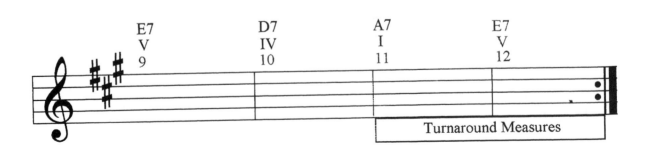

Section Two

CREATING THE "GROOVE"

Blues "shuffle" rhythm

Blues jams

Blues open position • Quick change IV change

Single note shuffle • Double note variation

Tritones – part one • Slow blues one • Slow blues two

Tritones – part two • Upbeat rhythm pattern

Blues shuffle – closed position

Blues "Shuffle" Rhythm

The distinguishing trademark of the "blues" is found in its rhythm; specifically, the rhythmic and stimulating "trip-let" beat called **shuffle rhythm**. Authentic 12-bar blues shuffle rhythm, which is at the heart of blues music, first became popular with blues musicians in the early 1920s. T-Bone Walker, the original Texas blues legend, created a unique guitar style by combining shuffle rhythms with a simplistic five-note pentatonic scale. Shuffle-based tunes like B.B. King's "Everyday I Have the Blues" and Robert Johnson's "Dust My Broom" are so fundamentally stimulating that even the novice listenter will find themselves tapping their foot in response to the beat.

THE "SHUFFLE FEEL"

The *shuffle feel* is just that – a feeling. It is developed by slightly changing the straight ahead 4/4 beat. One of the simplest and most common blues shuffle patterns is a rhythmic three-note riff played on the bass strings. It is played with down strokes heavily dampened by the picking hand and played in time with the bass guitar and bass drum. Whatever the tempo, this pattern forms the basis of the "shuffle feel".

THE "BLUES GROOVE"

The blues feel is all about playing the **groove**; that unique off-the-beat rhythmic pulse that defines blues music. This important aspect of blues rhythm applies to both the rhythm (chords) and the lead (scales). It is impossible to play blues riffs, licks and solos if the phrasing of the notes does not properly lay over the shuffle rhythm pattern. We encourage you to listen to the accompanying CD, and be sure to practice all examples demonstrated in this book against one of the rhythm tracks. Without the *groove*, your lead licks will be nothing but a series of notes.

Division of the Beat

We begin our study of blues rhythm by analyzing the components that create the blues groove. They are: tempo, time signature, note or rest value and accented beats. The blues groove is all about tempo, rhythm and timing. Within every musical composition, there is a basic pulse called the beat that organizes and drives the music. The term "beat" is most properly defined as music's basic unit of time measurement – the beats are the individual pulses. A rhythm will have a steady pattern of accented (emphasized) and unaccented (weaker) beats. This pattern of regulated pulses, or beats, in a musical composition is called "meter". The terms *meter* and *time* are interchangeable.

ILLUSTRATION ONE
QUARTER NOTES

By dividing one measure written in 4/4 time into four equal parts, we create four **quarter notes** – one played on each beat. *Count: one, two, three, four.*

EIGHTH NOTES

By dividing a quarter note (one beat) in half, we create two **eighth notes** – two notes that are played in the span of one beat. *Count: one and two and three and four and.*

EIGHTH NOTE TRIPLETS

By dividing each beat into three subdivisions, we create an **eighth note triplet** – three notes that are played in the span of one beat. *Count: one-e-and, two-e-and, three-e-and, four-e-and.*

ILLUSTRATION TWO/THREE/FOUR

In these three illustrations, we demonstrate the tonal character and feel of playing in quarter notes, eighth notes and eighth note triplets.

Audio Illustration: Listen to these examples and play along with the band.

BLUES SHUFFLE RHYTHM

ILLUSTRATION ONE
DIVISION OF THE BEAT

COUNT ONE   ONE - - -AND   ONE - -E - - AND

ILLUSTRATION TWO
PLAYING QUARTER NOTES

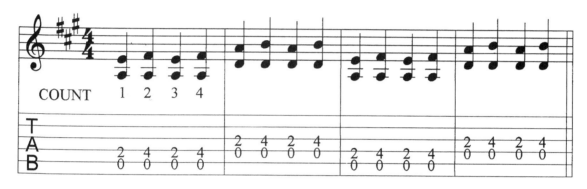

ILLUSTRATION THREE
PLAYING STRAIGHT EIGHTH NOTES

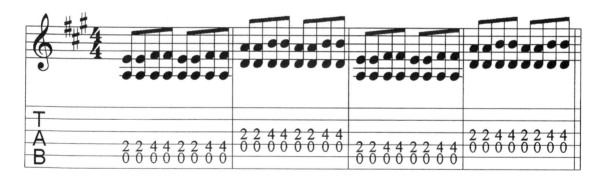

ILLUSTRATION FOUR
PLAYING EIGHTH NOTE TRIPLETS

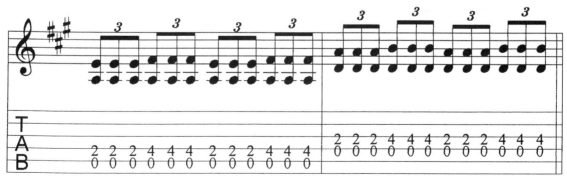

COUNT   1 e and   2 e and   3 e and   4 e and

Shuffle "Triplet" Rhythm Pattern

Capturing the shuffle beat in written notation can become most confusing. There are many different ways it may be written, and a complete dissertation on the subject goes beyond the scope of this book. In our written illustrations in this book, we will use the more common method of writing the shuffle beat – the double eighth note. We will also demonstrate several other methods of placing the shuffle beat in written notation. We strongly suggest that you listen to the rhythm patterns played on the *Audio Illustration CD* tracks and develop the *feel* for this dynamic aspect of playing blues.

ILLUSTRATION ONE
TRIPLETS

Any group of three notes in which each note is played with the same time value (equal duration), and the same accent, is called a *triplet*. These three notes are linked with a curved line called a *slur* (similar to a tie line) and the number 3 is written over the top or at the bottom. Triplets are usually used to describe the effect of three notes being played in the space of one beat. Triplet notation is a necessary device in music, because there is no other way to indicate dividing a time value into thirds. In 4/4 time, where one beat equals one quarter note, a triplet of eighth notes represent three notes played in the span of one beat. Musicians often count triplets using the term: *one trip-let, two trip-let, etc.*

ILLUSTRATION TWO
TIED EIGHTH NOTES WRITTEN AS A "QUARTER NOTE/EIGHTH NOTE"

The blues shuffle rhythm pattern is created by playing only the first and last eighth note of each set of eighth note triplets. The second eighth note is tied to the first. When two notes are tied, you play only the first, and let it sustain for the combination of the two.

ILLUSTRATION THREE
THE LOOK – THE FEEL

Placing the blues feel in written notation is most difficult. The *feel* of the shuffle defies notation. It is a subtlness of expression, a slight time elongation of the first note and a slight pause on the second note of the eight-note pair. It is only by carefully listening to the blues shuffle that you may fully comprehend this subtle difference between notes. In *Illustration Three*, we show in the first measure, in notation, how the notes are most commonly written; and in the second measure we show, in notation, how the two notes should feel when played.

SHUFFLE TRIPLETS

ILLUSTRATION ONE
EIGHTH NOTE TRIPLETS

One - Trip - let
Two - Trip - let

Tie

Trip - 0 - let

ILLUSTRATION TWO
TIED EIGHTH NOTES WRITTEN AS QUARTER NOTES-EIGHTH NOTES

Trip - 0 - let

Trip - 0 - let

ILLUSTRATION THREE
THE LOOK – THE FEEL

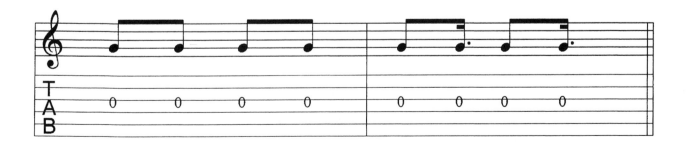

CREATING THE GROOVE

Blues Jam One
The Blues in the Open Position

The shuffle pattern used in "Blues Jam One" is one of the most common blues rhythm sequences. It can be played over all three chords in a blues chord progression. "Blues Jam One" is in the key of *A* major, and the chords are: *A7, D7* and *E7*. The notes that form these three chords are found within the *A* major scale. This basic rhythmic phrase is played off the root note of the chord (this also applies to other keys). In this example, the pattern moves across the strings, starting with the first note of each pattern on the root note of each new chord.

We start the bass note pattern on the open fifth string, which is the note *A*. This is the root note of the tonic chord, *A* (the **I** chord). When the same fingering pattern is moved up one string to the open *D* string, it covers the sub-dominant *D* chord (**IV** chord). When the fingering pattern is moved down to the open sixth string, the pattern covers the dominant *E7* chord (**V7** chord). Chuck Berry's "Johnny B. Goode" and Stevie Ray Vaughn's "Look at Little Sister" are good examples of this familiar fixture in blues rhythm patterns.

CREATING DYNAMICS

The sound of the blues shuffle varies from artist to artist and from song to song. Playing the same notes with different dynamics can create a *feel* unique to the individual performance. Just a change in the power of the pick hitting the strings will create a change in the sound produced. Implementing left-hand *bounce*, relaxing the pressure on the strings in between the down strokes, will cause a rise and fall in the dynamics that adds interest to the music. Dampening the strings to reduce overtones is a fundamental technique in creating authentic blues shuffle rhythm. This is accomplished by resting the palm (called a *palm mute*) of the picking hand on the strings close to the bridge as the notes are played. Changing the amount of pressure on the strings changes the effect of the rhythmic pulse.

THE COUNT-OFF

At the beginning of each Blues Jam, we incorporate a musical device called a *count off*. A count-off is a verbal instruction which enables musicians to know when to commence playing. The cadence of the count-off is used to establish the correct tempo.

BLUES JAM ONE
The Blues in the Open Position

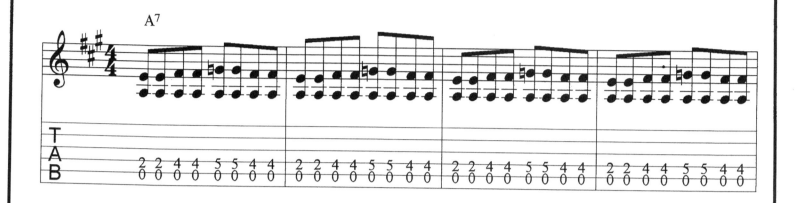

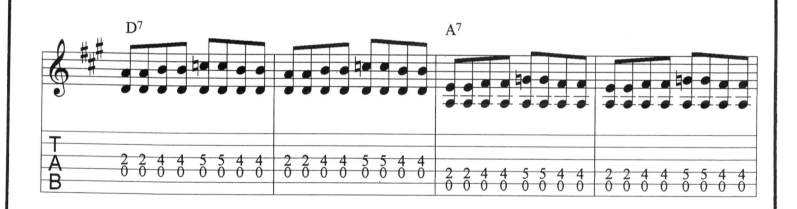

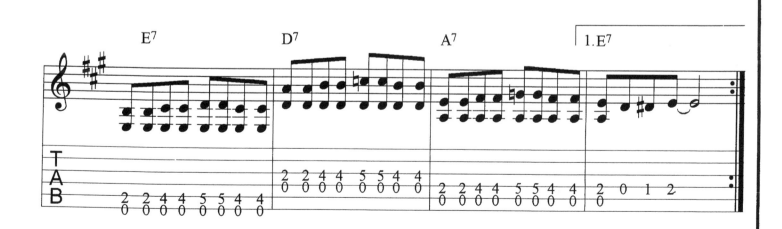

Blues Jam Two
Quick IV Change
Blues Progression
Open Position Variation on Blues Jam One

The most common 12-bar blues progression makes a change to the subdominant (**IV**) chord in measure two. This early change to the IV chord is called the *quick-change* blues progression. In this familiar blues pattern, the root of the chord is a drone note that continues to ring while the upper voice moves between the 5th, 6th and flat 7th chord tones.

AUDIO ILLUSTRATION

On the first and second time through, the band guitarist plays the rhythm pattern. We encourage you to play along with him. On the second, third and fourth time through, the band guitarist does not play the rhythm bass note pattern. This will give you the opportunity to play the part.

BLUES JAM TWO

Quick Change – Shuffle Rhythm

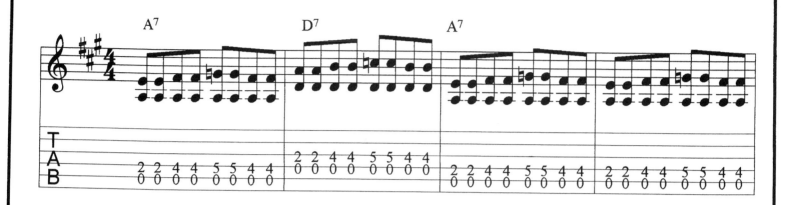

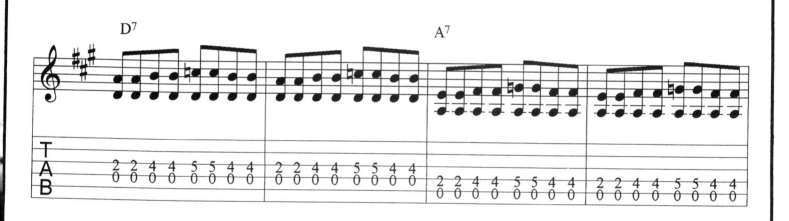

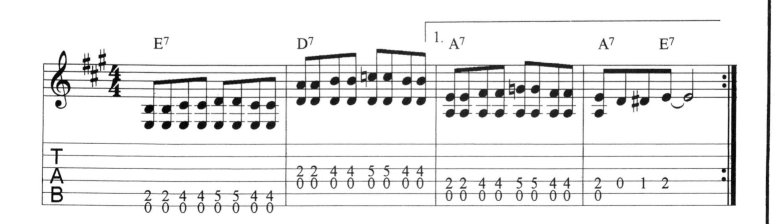

Blues Jam Three
Open Position

"Blues Jam Three" is a variation of "Blues Jam Two". In this example, the upper voice is played off the beat. This technique is typical of Jimmy Reed's, "Bright Lights Big City". As with many rhythm patterns in blues music, the same fingering (picking) sequence is used throughout the arrangement. The sequences are moved to different strings in order to follow the chord patterns. This arrangement uses a two-bar turnaround which incorporates another common blues device, a descending bass note pattern (eleventh measure).

PICKUP NOTES

"Blues Jam Three" begins with an eighth note placed in front of the first complete measure. This note is called a *pickup* note. It is an eighth note and played on the up-beat before the first beat of the first measure. The count: **and . . . one**. Play the pickup note on the **and**.

TURNAROUNDS

A good blues player must know the melodic phrases – the *introduction* (intros) and *turnarounds* that define blues music. The word *turnaround* is a term used in music to describe a musical phrase played at the end of a piece (the last measure, or in some instances, the last two measures). It creates tension, because it sounds incomplete and leads the ear back to the first measure of the chorus. A good turnaround device is the dominant (**V7**) chord, and notes of the scale that harmonize the dominant chord.

TAGS

A *tag* is defined as a short musical statement, usually one or two beats, that normally occurs at the end of the twelfth measure. It may either be a series of notes, or a cluster of chords. Tags are always embedded in the turnaround phrases.

AUDIO ILLUSTRATION

On the first time through, the band guitarist plays the rhythm pattern. We encourage you to play along with them. On the second, third and fourth time through, the guitarist does not play the rhythm bass note patterns – so you may play the part and enjoy the thrill of creating the *blues groove!*

BLUES JAM THREE
Single Note Shuffle

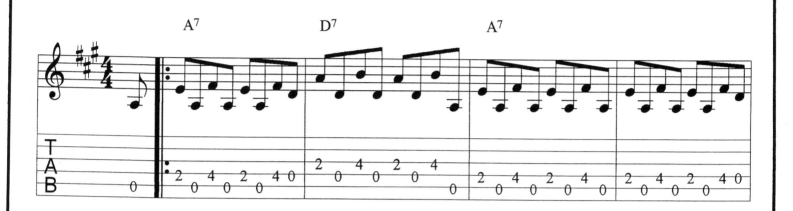

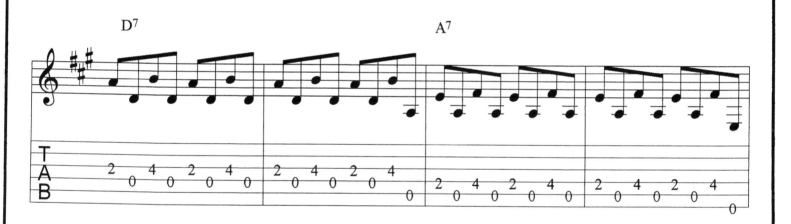

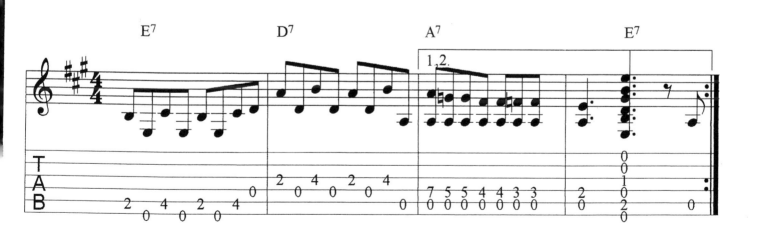

Blues Jam Four

Variations on the Bass Note Pattern

The use of dominant seventh chords in blues rhythm patterns first appeared in the 1920's, when blues musicians began using the pentatonic scale (example: In the key of *A* major – *A7, D7, E7*). The conventional tension release of the dominant seventh chord back to the tonic was abandoned. This non-classical approach to chord harmony created the open, unsettled and moody feel that has become the hallmark of blues melodic phrasing. Today, blues guitarists incorporate extended dominant chord tones (the 9th and 13th) of the scale, which adds a subtle and jazzier refinement of blues chord harmony.

"Blues Jam Four" utilizes a more complex *double stop* (double note) rhythm pattern. The twelfth measure turnaround uses a very stylish quick chord change: *F9* to *E9* (both dominant chords). This chord pattern is a very effective turnaround phrase.

---PLAYING TIP---
It takes a variety of articulation, rythm and dynamics to give life to a blues riff.

BLUES JAM FOUR
Double Note Variation

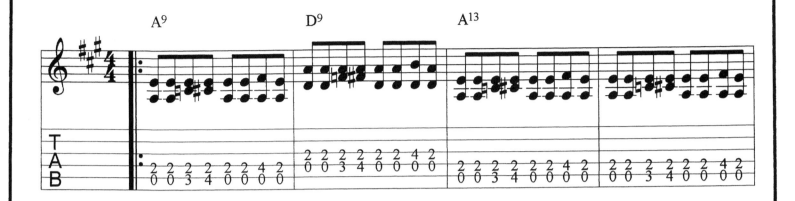

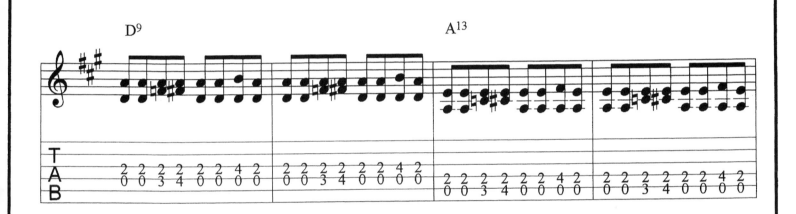

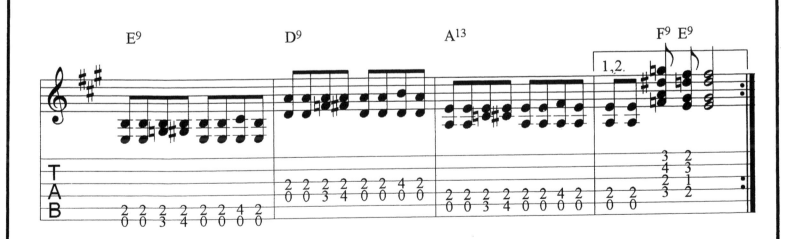

Blues Jam Five

"Tritones" – Part One

DOMINANT CHORD TRITONES

A *tritone* is an interval of three whole-steps and divides an octave in half. It creates a unique sound, and in chord construction, forms a two-note chord shape around which hundreds of classic blues licks have been created. Dominant chords contain a tritone interval consisting of the 3rd and b7th degrees. The third degree establishes the chord as major (a flat third creates a minor chord). The inclusion of the flat seventh establishes the dominant sound.

TRITONES – THE MAGIC BLUES CHORDS

In the key of *A* major, the three primary chords played as sevenths (*A7*, *D7* and *E7*) reduced to their tritones, appear on the third and fourth strings – one fret apart. (Example: The *A7* tritone is at the fifth and sixth fret, the *D7* tritone, a half-step (one fret) lower is on the fourth and fifth fret, and the *E7's* tritone is a half-step above the *A7*, at the sixth and seventh fret. The same finger pattern, moved between three frets, produces the three primary chords of the key of which the song is played, a unique phenmenon! Another oddity – move between the tonic chord *A7* and the subdominant *D7* (one fret), reverses the relationship of the third and seventh tones.) Thirds become flat sevenths. Flat sevenths become thirds! Same two notes, same interval, different names, two different chords!

TRITONE PATTERNS: CIRCLE OF FOURTHS – CIRCLE OF FIFTHS

Tritones played as *closed* chord shapes (no open strings) are *movable* chord forms and they may be played at each fret. A tritone chord form does not move chromatically like the barr chords. Tritones move in 4th and 5th intervals, musical devices called the *circle of fourths* and *circle of fifths*.

In the key of *A*, the subdominant *D7* (**IV**), one fret lower than the tonic *A7* (**I**), on the fretboard, is not one chromatic tone lower (*Ab*), it is a fourth interval lower (*D*), **circle of fourths**. The dominant chord *E7* (**V**), one fret higher than the tonic, is not one chromatic tone higher (*A#*), it is a fifth interval higher (*E*), **circle of fifths**.

How can you easily determine upon which fret to play a tritone chord pattern? Let's assume you know the *A* tritone, the tonic (**I**) chord in the key of *A* major, is located on the fifth and sixth frets. Tritones move up through the musical alphabet in fifth intervals, circle of fifths. For each fret up the fretboard, count up five notes in the scale. (Example: The *A* tritone is located at the fifth and sixth frets. Move this position up one fret. The next tritone becomes *E*. Count up five letters in the alphabet – *A B C D E*. Move another fret, count up five letters – *E F G A B*. At the seventh and eighth frets, the tritone becomes *B*. For each fretboard down the neck, count up four notes in the scale. (Example: The *A* tritone is located at the fifth fret. Move the chord shape down one fret and you have moved up only four letters in the musical alphabet.

For each fret back or down the fretboard, count up four notes in the scale (circle of fourths). (*Example:* the *A* tritone, fifth and sixth frets, lowered one fret becomes *D*. Count four notes from *A* – *A B C D*, circle of fourths!) One fret lower, four notes in the scale, the tritone created at the third and fourth fret is *G*.

BLUES JAM FIVE

"Tritones" – Part One

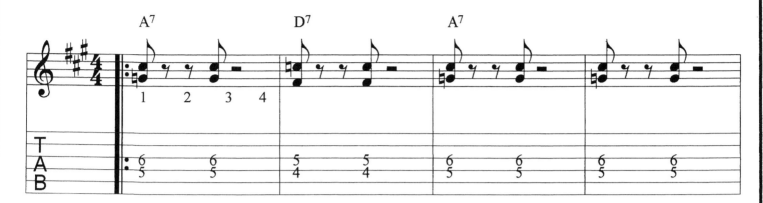

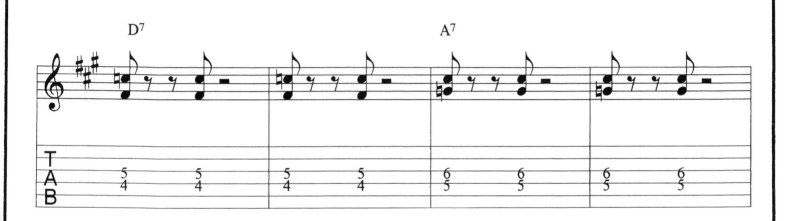

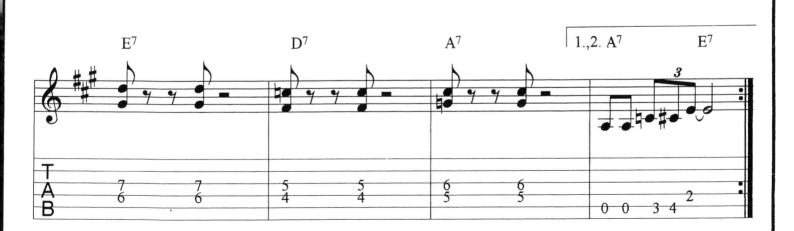

Blues Jam Six
"Slow Blues" Rhythm Patterns

"Blues Jam Six" is an example of a rhythm pattern that works well over a slow tempo blues song. It is a pattern often played by the horn section in a blues band. T-Bone Walker is credited with creating this style of blues rhythm. Slow blues *horn* phrases are two measure phrases. And in a typical 12-bar arrangement, this results in six phrases. The only variation would be the last two measures, or the turnaround. This type of rhythm phrases utilizes a mix of altered chords. It also utilizes a three-note chord shape. The tonal effect is created by sliding each shape from one position to the next – a two-fret movement. Notice how the fingering for the *A6*, when moved back two frets, creates *A9*! The same principle applies to the *D6-D9* and the *E6-E9* chords.

GRACE NOTES – SLIDES

In this pattern, we introduce a phrasing device called a *slide*. A slide sounds like a slur. A slur is a quick tone played as the fingers (without releasing pressure on the strings) slide to the host note(s).

In tablature, slide notes appear on their appropriate string (represented by the horizontal lines of the tab staff), as a number indicating the fret where each note is to be played. Short lines placed before or after a number indicate a slide. Play the first note and slide up or down to the next pitch.

NOTE: It is possible to combine "Blues Jam Six" and "Blues Jam Seven" for an additional pattern. Also, this pattern may be played with "Blues Jam Five". Try it!

BLUES JAM SIX
Slow Blues One

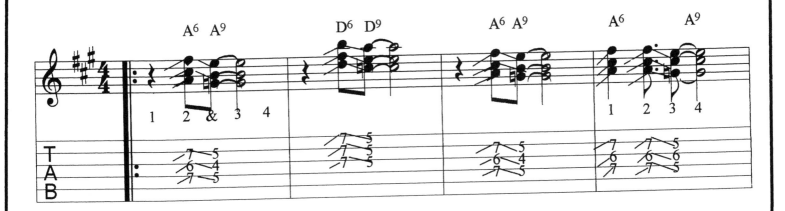

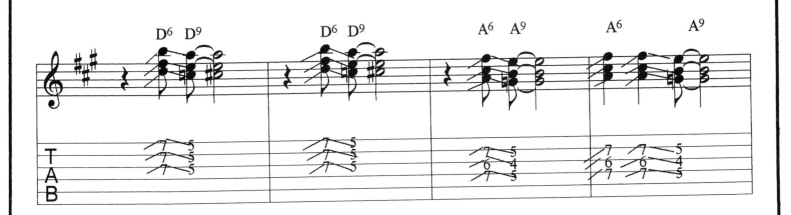

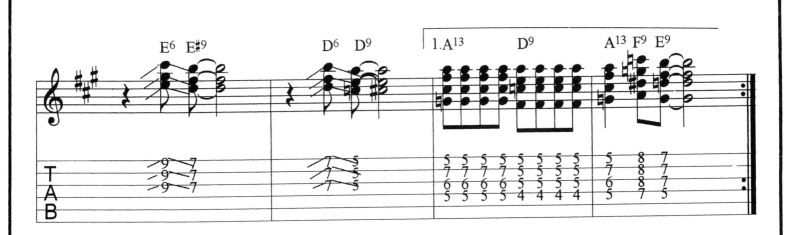

BLUES JAM SEVEN
Slow Blues Two

"Blues Jam Seven" is in the key of *A* major, and the chords are *A9, D9, E9*. It is a great pattern to use in the hornless rhythm section. This type of progression provides a smooth rhythm bed for singers and instrumentalists. The trick is to play with ease and make the chord changes smoothly. The two bars of metronome after the count off are left for practicing introductions and favorite licks. Practice turnarounds and endings with bars 11 and 12.

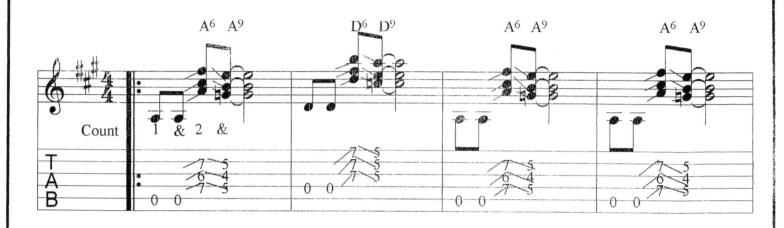

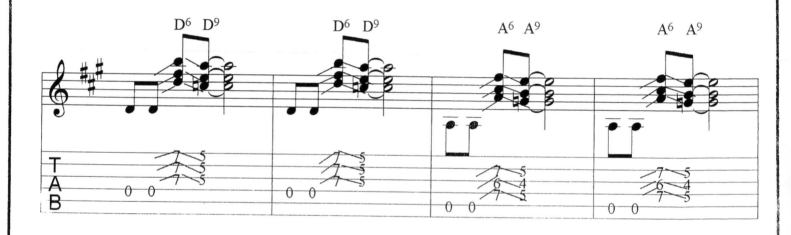

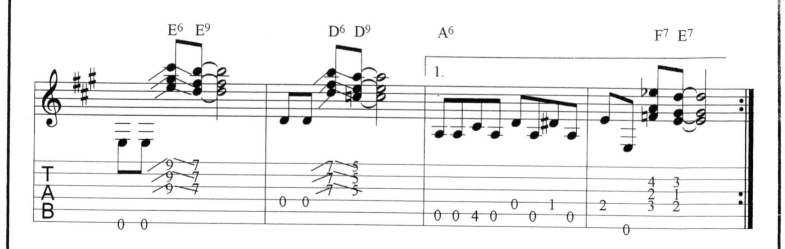

BLUES JAM EIGHT

"Tritones" – Part Two

"Blues Jam Eight" expands upon our study of tritone rhythm patterns. Again, this is an effective pattern for use in slow blues songs. The two bars of metronome after the count off are left for practicing introductions and favorite licks. Practice turnarounds and endings with bars 11 and 12.

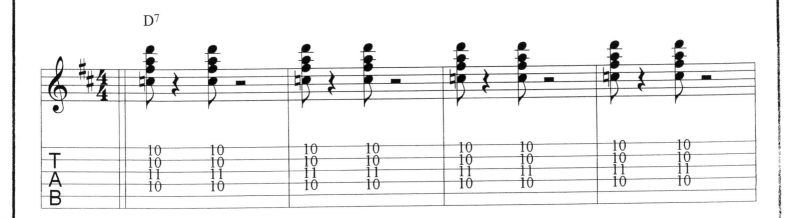

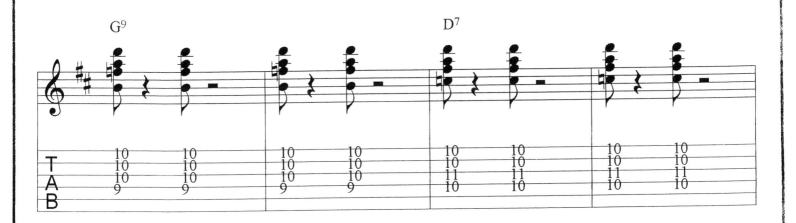

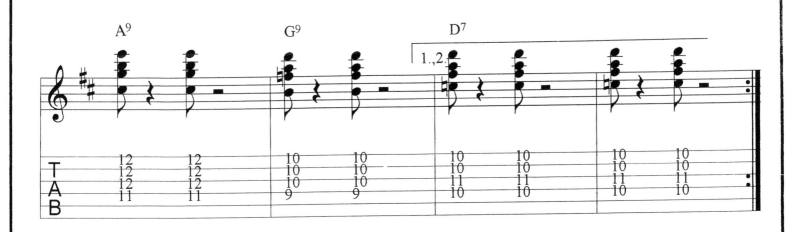

Blues Jam Nine
Upbeat Rhythm Pattern

One commonly used blues rhythm pattern is called the *up-beat* pattern, or piano style pattern. In this rhythm pattern, the pianist's left hand plays chords on the downbeat, and the right hand plays chords on the up beat (*off beat*). In a blues band, the bass plays the down beat – on the count (one, two, etc.); and the guitar plays chords on the off beat, or up-beat (and, and, etc.). The rhythm pattern is still a triplet shuffle-trip-o-let, trip-o-let. The bass plays the first part of the triplet. The guitar plays the last part.

The feel for the pattern can be obtained by keeping the right arm (picking hand) moving in unison with the foot-down on the down beat, up on the up-beat, missing the strings on the downbeat, strumming the strings on the up-beat, sometimes call the *backbeat*. Some guitarists prefer to come down with the heal of the picking hand, the bottom edge, and lightly striking the bridge of the guitar on the downbeat, then raising the hand off the bridge and strumming the strings with a short up-stroke on the up-beat. Either way is a good approach, experiment and find the one with which you feel most comfortable.

DOMINANT CHORDS

It is common in blues to play dominant chords (example: A7, A9, A13). These dominant chord voicings add tension and change the texture and sophistication of the music. A dominant chord is a four tone chord. It is created by adding a flat seventh of the scale to the chord triad. *A9* is created by also adding the ninth note of the scale to a dominant chord. *A13* is created by adding the thirteenth note of the scale to a dominant chord. (Note: The flatted 7th must remain in the 9th and 13th chords. In dominant chords, the 5th is usually omitted.)

BLUES JAM NINE

UP-BEAT PATTERN

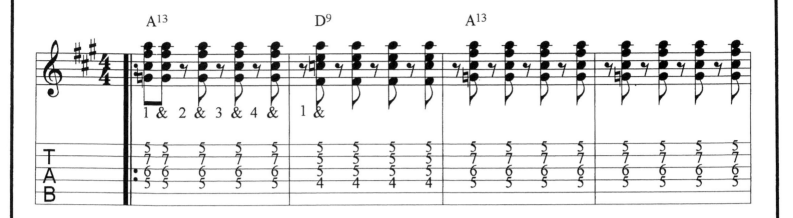

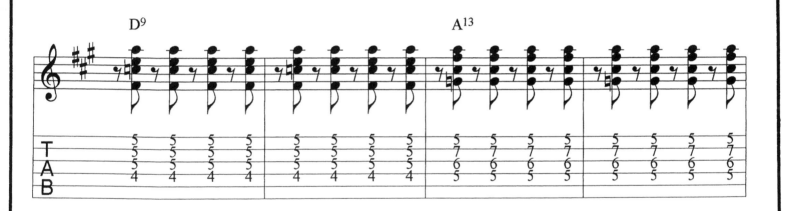

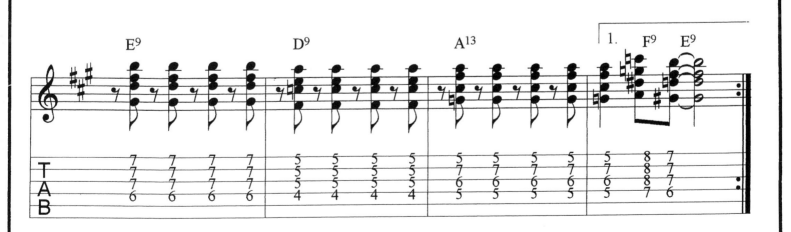

BLUES JAM TEN

Blues Shuffle – Closed Position

"Blues Jam Ten" is a repeat of the single note pattern used in "Blues Jam Two". But in this arrangement, we are playing the pattern at the fifth position (fifth fret). It incorporates fretted notes – no open strings – and is, therefore, moveable. (*Example:* If the same fingering patterns are played at the eighth fret, the arrangement would be in the key of *C* major. At the third fret, the arrangement would be in the key of *G* major.)

Use the last two bars to practice endings and tags.

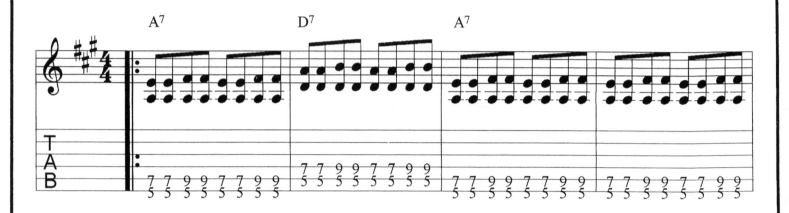

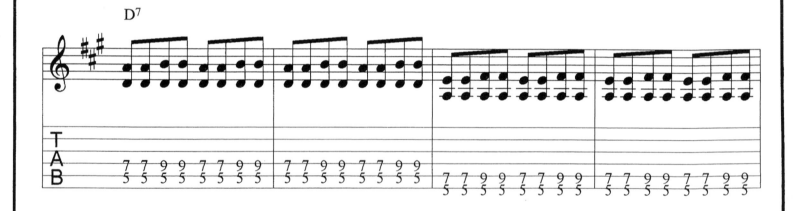

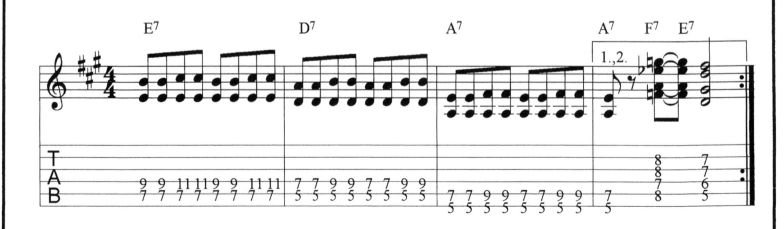

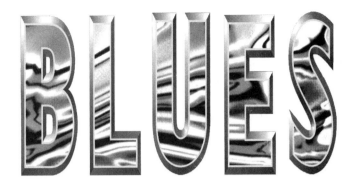

Everything about Playing BLUES

Section Three

SCALE MANAGEMENT

C-A-G-E-D system of scale-chord patterns

The C-A-G-E-D sequence of scales

Box position scales

How About Tuning Your Guitar?

Have you encountered problems tuning the guitar? Electronic tuners are in vogue these days, and that's great if, when needed, the battery isn't dead and you can find the magical little black box. Tuners provide either a tone or digital readout for each string, and it does take the guesswork out of the process of tuning the instrument to pitch. But what happens when you don't have one of these modern marvels? In the old days, we used a "tuning fork", or in the *really* old days (God forbid), a "pitch pipe".

Most anyone that plays the guitar has mastered the task of tuning string to string. However, there is the problem of the initial pitch from which all the other strings are tuned. If you do not have an electric tuner, tuning fork or pitch pipe, here's a simple solution. Pick up the phone and listen to the dial tone. Most phone companies use the pitch of A 440 for their dial tone, so you can tune the guitar's fifth string to your phone!

Another tip – when you do not have a beginning pitch, release the pressure on all the strings – let them flop on the fretboard. In this manor, you know that all the strings must be tightened (pulled up to proper pitch). Now, bring the tension up on the sixth string until you feel it sounds okay. You can now tune string to string, and almost always, you will be very close to proper pitch. In fact, most likely, you will be tuned slightly below pitch and you won't have over stressed the first and second strings and break them by tuning too high. *Something to think about.*

Scale Management

Proper management of scales is an art form few guitarists fully master. It really comes down to knowing what to play, and what not to play. Proper management of these most fundamental tools of improvisation will, not in themselves, neccessarily make you an exceptional player, only one that does not play bad notes. Exceptional players take the correct notes and create great music . . . another art form!

Why learn scales? You do not play scales to create solos, you manipulate the notes of a scale to create original melodies. Critics lament that scales are boring, lifeless, contrived and musically ineffective. To say that scales are limiting and hamper creativity is to miss the point. We manage scales so we may play with no wrong notes, or notes that "hurt" the ears, so to speak. Focus on scale management and the application of scales so that you may play with confidence.

SCALE PATTERN DEVELOPMENT

As we have demonstrated, notes do not appear at random on the fretbord. Every aspect of music as applied to the guitar is systematic and predictable. Notes may be organized into various types of scales which provide order and fingering patterns can be developed.

On the guitar, there are countless finger patterns possible for any given scale. Therefore, it is desirable to reduce the options to a few more manageable forms. There are essentially three ways we can play scales on the fretboard: a LINEAR, lengthwise movement; a POSITION, a sized pattern of tones that move diagonally across the neck, also called a "box"; and a combination of the two – a ZIGZAG movement.

The blues guitarist must be able to move spontaneously in any direction, play in every key, and be able to play at any position on the fretboard. To accomplish this, we must be able to effectively play scales from more than one scale pattern. In the course of our study of blues, we will explore *linear* patterns, *position* patterns, and *zigzag* scale patterns.

SCALE POSITION "BOX" SCALE PATTERN

We will begin our study by first concentrating on the *position* form of playing scales. A position encompasses all notes of a given scale placed normally within five frets. There are five "open" positions. These are scales played within the first four frets and utilize notes produced by the open strings (*E A D G B E*). And there are five moveable "closed" positions in which there are no open string notes. A fixed position, open or closed, is referred to as a "box" position.

The *C A G E D* System
of Scale-Chord Patterns

THE *C A G E D* SYSTEM

There are several scale finger patterns in common usage. They are patterns developed by individual guitarists to facilitate their unique style of playing. The *C A G E D* system of scale management relates to scale patterns that overlay the five basic chord forms found in the "open position". The open chords *C A G E* and *D*. These five open chords, when moved up the neck and barred with the first finger, become "closed chord forms". These closed chords are called "barr chords". (*Illustration Two*).

ILLUSTRATION ONE
"OPEN" MAJOR CHORDS

Here, we present the five "open" major chords upon which the five *C A G E D* scale patterns are constructed.

ILLUSTRATION TWO
"CLOSED" MAJOR CHORDS

Here, we show the five open major chords played as "closed" moveable barr chords. In the closed position, each chord may be played at any fret, and ascends and descends chromatically in pitch through the entire 12 notes of the music alphabet. Black triangles indicate the root note(s) of each chord.

> **REMEMBER:** *The placement of the root note determines the name of the chord.*

The examples in this section can b e heard on the audio CD that is enclosed with our book, "Scales Over Chords".

CAGED CHORD FORMS

OPEN CHORDS

ILLUSTRATION ONE

Form One	Form Two	Form Three	Form Four	Form Five
C	**A**	**G**	**E**	**D**

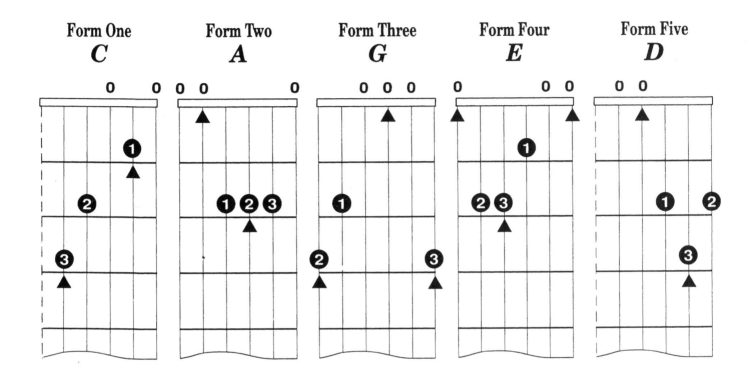

ILLUSTRATION TWO

CLOSED CHORDS (Moveable)

Form One	Form Two	Form Three	Form Four	Form Five

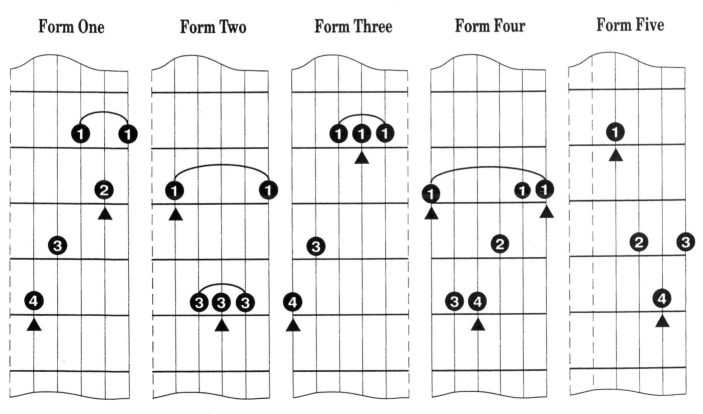

SCALE MANAGEMENT

The Box Position (Scales)

If you place your hand anywhere on the fretboard with one finger per fret, and play across the strings, you will cover two octaves of chromatic tones. This fixed position is called a **box position**. It is this box position that we utilize in the *C A G E D* system.

C Scale Pattern – Form One

ILLUSTRATION ONE

OPEN POSITION

On the following page, the left-hand diagrams present the open *C* chord form. Black triangles mark the chord's root note. It is from this *open chord form* that the overlying scale pattern acquires its name in the *C A G E D* system. In Illustration One, left-hand diagram, we show the open scale pattern that overlays this open chord form. We have indicated the chord fingering pattern that lies within the scale tones with black circles. Triangles mark the root note. The center diagram presents the *C* major scale in written notation and tab. We suggest that you strum the chord, then play the scale. Listen to how the scale harmonizes the chord. We suggest that you play all the notes in the scale diagram, for they complete the *boxed* position.

ILLUSTRATION TWO

CLOSED POSITION

In Illustration Two, right-hand diagram, we have placed the open *C* chord form at the second fret. The name of the chord is now *D* major. The diagram on the left is the *D* scale that overlays the chord. We include those notes that extended the scale to complete all of the notes found within the box. When playing this scale pattern, we are in the key of *D* major. Black triangles mark the scale's tonic note. Again, we have indicated the chord fingering pattern with black circles.

C SCALE PATTERN

ILLUSTRATION ONE

OPEN PATTERN

C SCALE

C CHORD: *C E G*

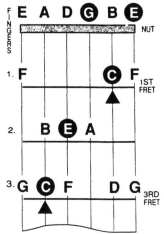

C MAJOR SCALE (Open)

ILLUSTRATION TWO

CLOSED "MOVEABLE" PATTERN

D SCALE

D CHORD: *D F# A*

D MAJOR SCALE (Moveable)

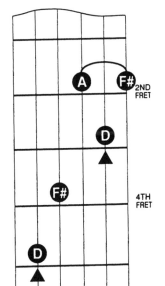

A Scale Pattern – Form Two

ILLUSTRATION ONE

OPEN POSITION

On the following page, the left-hand diagrams present the open *A* chord form. Black triangles mark the chord's root note. It is from this *open chord form* that the overlying scale pattern acquires its name in the *C A G E D* system. In Illustration One, left-hand diagram, we show the open scale pattern that overlays this open chord form. We have indicated the chord fingering pattern that lies within the scale tones with black circles. Triangles mark the root note. The center diagram presents the *A* major scale in written notation and tab. We suggest that you strum the chord, then play the scale. Listen to how the scale harmonizes the chord. We suggest that you play all the notes in the scale diagram, for they complete the *box* position.

ILLUSTRATION TWO

CLOSED POSITION

In Illustration Two, right-hand diagram, we have placed the open *A* chord form at the third fret. The name of the chord is now *C* major. The diagram on the left is the *C* scale that overlays the chord. We include those notes that extended the scale to complete all of the notes found within the box. When playing this scale pattern, we are in the key of *C* major. Black triangles mark the scale's tonic note. Again, we have indicated the chord fingering pattern with black circles.

A SCALE PATTERN

ILLUSTRATION ONE

OPEN PATTERN

This is the second of our five open scale patterns. It encompasses, within the open position, all notes of the *A* Major scale. It is called the *A* pattern, because it overlays the open string *A* chord form.

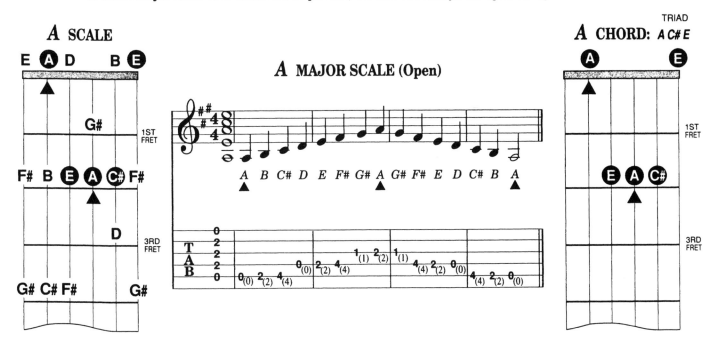

ILLUSTRATION TWO

CLOSED "MOVEABLE" PATTERN

This is the second of our five closed scale patterns. It encompasses all notes of the scale associated with the moveable *A* chord form. The Tonic note (name of the scale), is located on the fifth and third strings. The Tonic note establishes the Key or name of the scale at each fret.

G Scale Pattern – Form Three

ILLUSTRATION ONE

OPEN POSITION

On the following page, the left-hand diagrams present the open *G* chord form. Black triangles mark the chord's root note. It is from this *open chord form* that the overlying scale pattern acquires its name in the *C A G E D* system. In Illustration One, left-hand diagram, we show the open scale pattern that overlays this open chord form. We have indicated the chord fingering pattern that lies within the scale tones with black circles. Triangles mark the root note. The center diagram presents the *G* major scale in written notation and tab. We suggest that you strum the chord, then play the scale. Listen to how the scale harmonizes the chord. We suggest that you play all the notes in the scale diagram, for they complete the *box* position.

ILLUSTRATION TWO

CLOSED POSITION

In Illustration Two, right-hand diagram, we have placed the open *G* chord form at the second fret. The name of the chord is now *A* major. The diagram on the left is the *A* scale that overlays the chord. We include those notes that extended the scale to complete all of the notes found within the box. When playing this scale pattern, we are in the key of *A* major. Black triangles mark the scale's tonic note. Again, we have indicated the chord fingering pattern with black circles.

G SCALE PATTERN

ILLUSTRATION ONE

OPEN PATTERN

This is the third of our five open scale patterns. It encompasses, within the open position, all notes of the G Major scale. It is called the G pattern, because it overlays the open string G chord form.

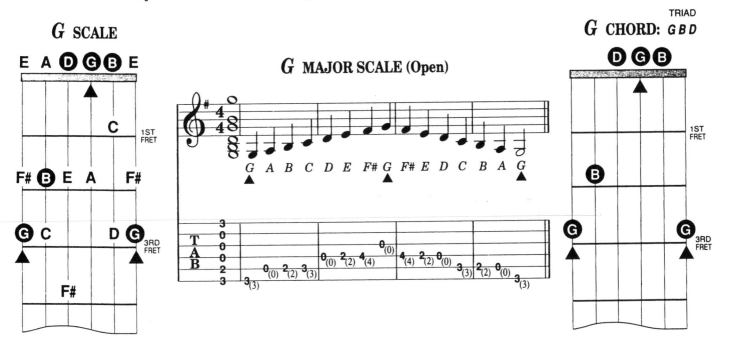

G SCALE

G MAJOR SCALE (Open)

G CHORD: *G B D*   TRIAD

ILLUSTRATION TWO

CLOSED "MOVEABLE" PATTERN

This is the third of our five closed scale patterns. It encompasses all notes of the scale associated with the moveable G chord form. The Tonic note (name of the scale), is located on the sixth, third and first strings. The Tonic note establishes the Key or name of the scale at each fret.

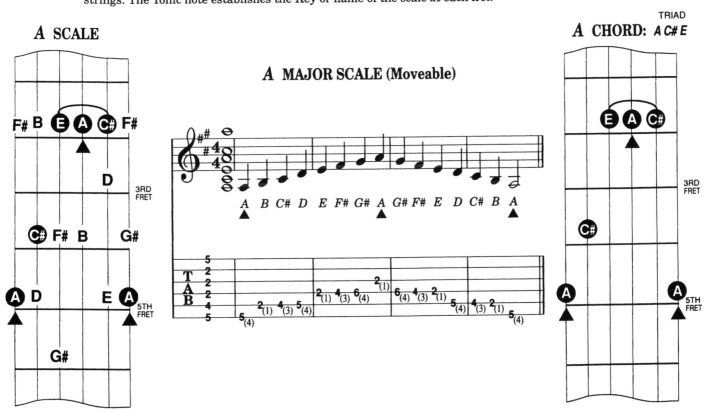

A SCALE

A MAJOR SCALE (Moveable)

A CHORD: *A C# E*   TRIAD

E Scale Pattern
– Form Four

ILLUSTRATION ONE

OPEN POSITION

On the following page, the right-hand diagrams present the open *E* chord form. Black triangles mark the chord's root note. It is from this *open chord form* that the overlying scale pattern acquires its name in the *C A G E D* system. In Illustration One, left-hand diagram, we show the open scale pattern that overlays this open chord form. We have indicated the chord fingering pattern that lies within the scale tones with black circles. Triangles mark the root note. The center diagram presents the *E* major scale in written notation and tab. We suggest that you strum the chord, then play the scale. Listen to how the scale harmonizes the chord. We suggest that you play all the notes in the scale diagram, for they complete the *box* position.

ILLUSTRATION TWO

CLOSED POSITION

In Illustration Two, right-hand diagram, we have placed the open *E* chord form at the third fret. The name of the chord is now *G* major. The diagram on the left is the *G* scale that overlays the chord. We include those notes that extended the scale to complete all of the notes found within the box. When playing this scale pattern, we are in the key of *G* major. Black triangles mark the scale's tonic note. Again, we have indicated the chord fingering pattern with black circles.

E SCALE PATTERN

ILLUSTRATION ONE

OPEN PATTERN

This is the fourth of our five open scale patterns. It encompasses, within the open position, all notes of the *E* Major scale. It is called the *E* pattern, because it overlays the open string *E* chord form.

ILLUSTRATION TWO

CLOSED "MOVEABLE" PATTERN

This is the fourth of our five closed scale patterns. It encompasses all notes of the scale associated with the moveable *E* chord form. The Tonic note (name of the scale), is located on the sixth, fourth and first strings. The Tonic note establishes the Key or name of the scale at each fret.

D Scale Pattern
– Form Five

ILLUSTRATION ONE

OPEN POSITION

On the following page, the right-hand diagrams present the open *D* chord form. Black triangles mark the chord's root note. It is from this *open chord form* that the overlying scale pattern acquires its name in the *C A G E D* system. In Illustration One, left-hand diagram, we show the open scale pattern that overlays this open chord form. We have indicated the chord fingering pattern that lies within the scale tones with black circles. Triangles mark the root note. The center diagram presents the *D* major scale in written notation and tab. We suggest that you strum the chord, then play the scale. Listen to how the scale harmonizes the chord. We suggest that you play all the notes in the scale diagram, for they complete the *box* position.

ILLUSTRATION TWO

CLOSED POSITION

In Illustration Two, right-hand diagram, we have placed the open *D* chord form at the second fret. The name of the chord is now *E* major. The diagram on the left is the *E* scale that overlays the chord. We include those notes that extended the scale to complete all of the notes found within the box. When playing this scale pattern, we are in the key of *E* major. Black triangles mark the scale's tonic note. Again, we have indicated the chord fingering pattern with black circles.

D SCALE PATTERN

ILLUSTRATION ONE

OPEN PATTERN

This is the fifth of our five open scale patterns. It encompasses, within the open position, all notes of the D Major scale. It is called the D pattern, because it overlays the open string D chord form.

ILLUSTRATION TWO

CLOSED "MOVEABLE" PATTERN

This is the fifth of our five closed scale patterns. It encompasses all notes of the scale associated with the moveable D chord form. The Tonic note (name of the scale), is located on the fourth and second strings. The Tonic note establishes the Key or name of the scale at each fret.

The "CAGED" Sequence of Chord-Scale Patterns

On the following pages, we show how the five individual *CAGED* chord patterns, when linked together, cover the entire range of the fretboard. Each pattern begins with the open chord position. Black triangles mark the root note of the chord. *Remember*: Each closed chord is moveable and the chord is named by the individual note of the chromatic scale upon which you begin the note sequence that forms the chord. The *C* chord fingering pattern, first fret, moved up two frets (*C C# D*), creates a *D* chord and the six scale patterns that overlay the chord will be in the key of *D*.

A POSITIVE THOUGHT

Perfect old technique, experiment with new ideas – learn something new every day!

ILLUSTRATION ONE
C FORM ONE

CAGED SEQUENCE

ILLUSTRATION TWO
A FORM TWO

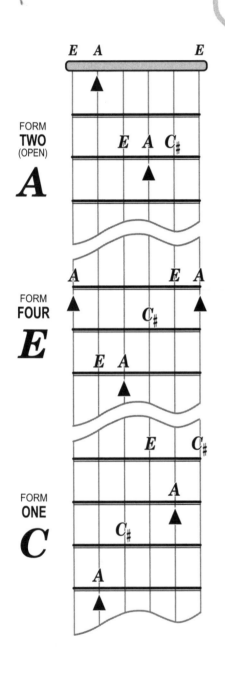

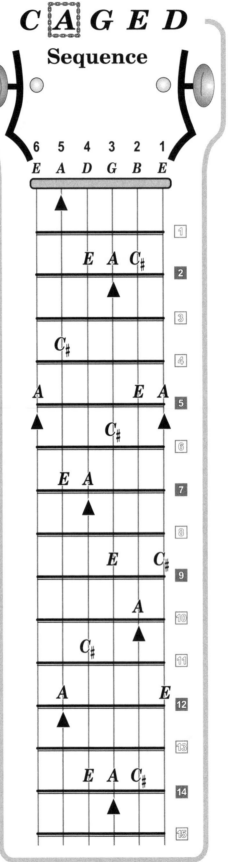

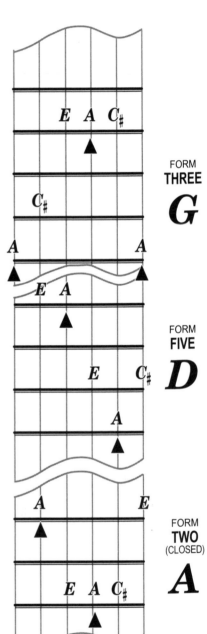

FORM
TWO
(OPEN)

A

FORM
FOUR

E

FORM
ONE

C

FORM
THREE

G

FORM
FIVE

D

FORM
TWO
(CLOSED)

A

CAGED SEQUENCE

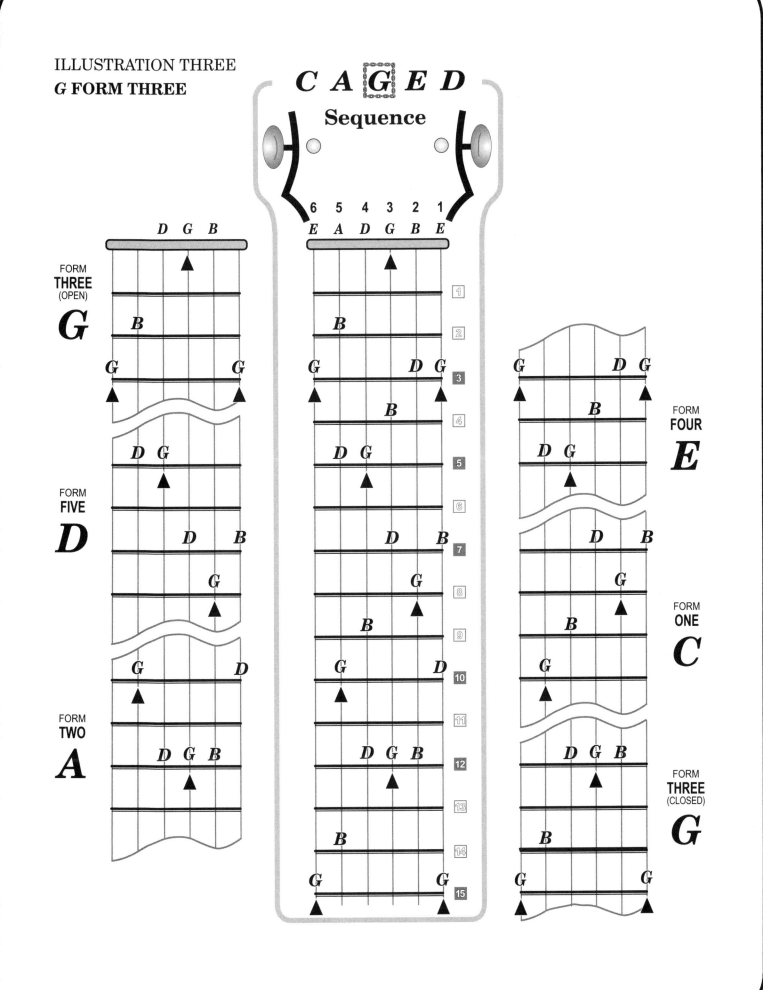

ILLUSTRATION THREE
G FORM THREE

CAGED SEQUENCE

ILLUSTRATION FOUR
***E* FORM FOUR**

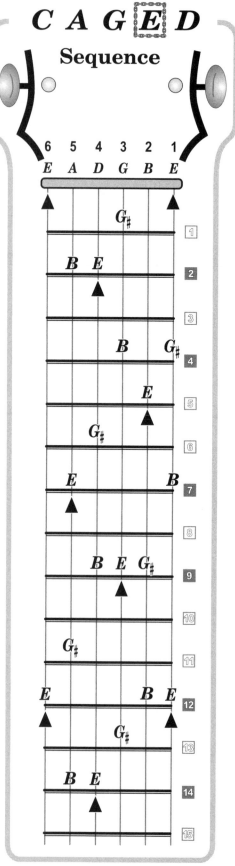

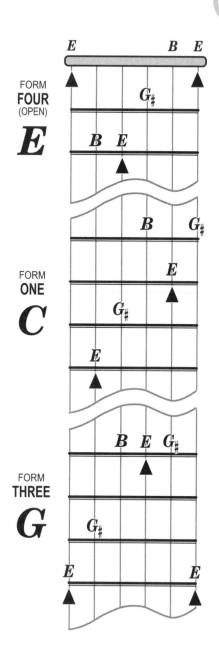

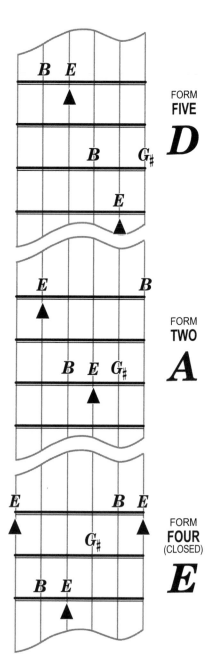

ILLUSTRATION FIVE
D FORM FIVE

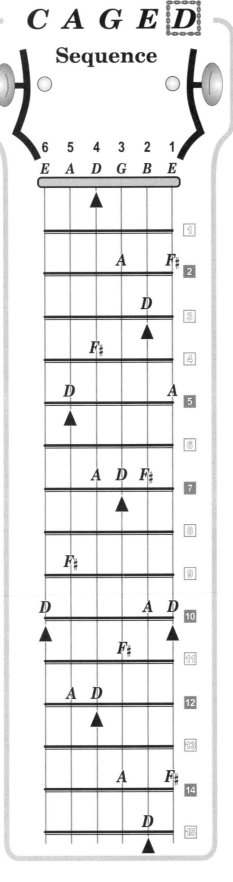

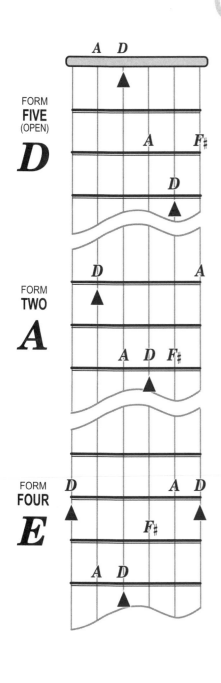

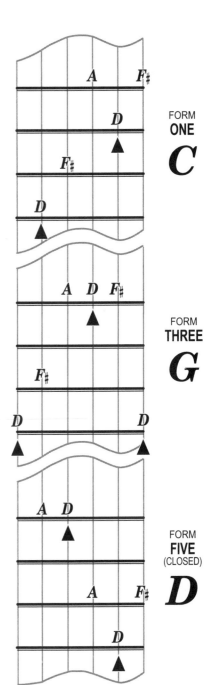

FORM
**FIVE
(OPEN)**

D

FORM
TWO

A

FORM
FOUR

E

FORM
ONE

C

FORM
THREE

G

FORM
**FIVE
(CLOSED)**

D

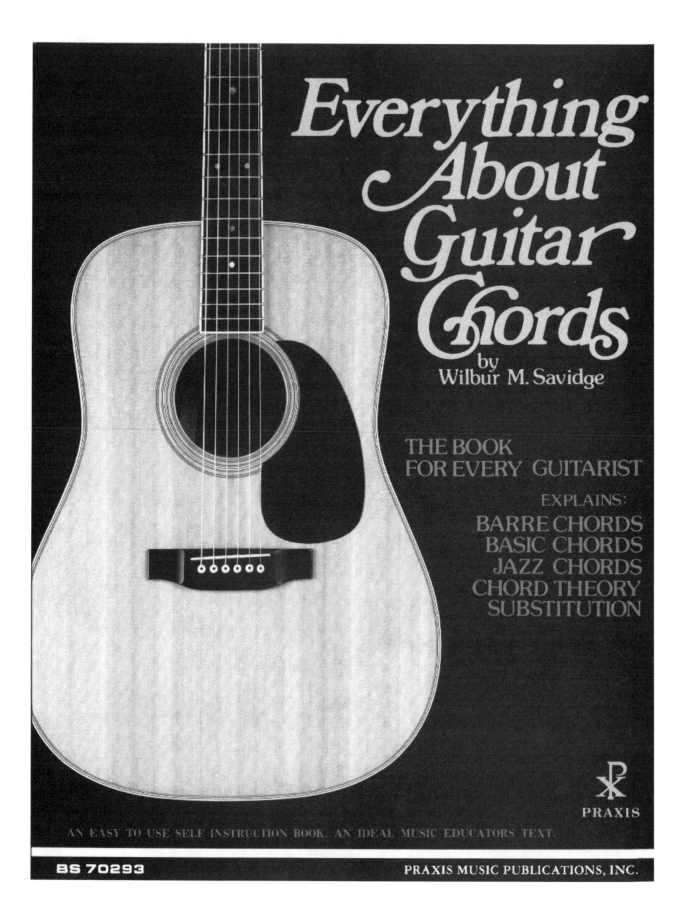

Six *C A G E D* Scale Patterns

Within the *C A G E D* system, there are numerous scale patterns that overlay each major chord form. We will concentrate on six; and they are – the **chromatic scale**, the **major scale**, the **major and minor pentatonic scales**, the **blues scale** and the **mixolydian scale**. Each scale pattern is related to the chord that it overlays and each scale is in the key of which the chord is named. (*Example:* If the chord is *G* major, then all six scales that overlay that chord form, will be *G* type scales.).

Each type of scale has a different application in music and seldom can we employ all six scales in the performance of a song. However, when you have mastered the six scales that overlay each of the five chord forms, you will have the technical skill to play a wide variety of music. It is important to remember that the difference between each scale is in the placement of the steps and half-steps that create each scale's tonality. (*Example:* In chord construction, by lowering the third of a major scale one fret – half-step – we create a minor chord of the same letter name.)

When you have mastered the six scales that overlay each chord form of the *C A G E D* system, you will then have the skill to play the same lick or riff in six positions on the guitar fretboard. Most blues guitarists eventually find one or two patterns they are comfortable with and use them to the exclusion of the other available patterns. You too, will come to prefer some patterns to the exclusion of others, but knowing how to play all five variations will allow you the freedom of expression and fretboard mobility that can only be achieved by mastering a variety of patterns. We strongly urge you to experiment with this concept. Play a favorite lick, and then figure it out in another of the *C A G E D* scale patterns. The ability to play in different positions on the neck is a must in order to play effectively and keep your music fresh.

Getting Started

Now, we present the five *movable* chord forms and the six movable scale patterns that overlay each chord. The notes between the black triangles represent one octave. The notes, above or below the octave, represent upper or lower scale tones that may be played without shifting position. In all of the following examples, we have chosen the key of *A*. This key is a favorite key used by blues musicians. Black triangles mark the root note of the chord (chord theory). In scale theory, this same note is referred to as the *tonic* note.

C Form

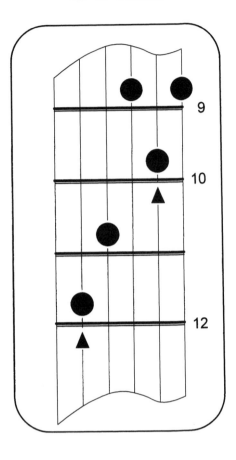

C Chord
Scale Patterns

On the following page, we present the first of the five chord forms – the *C* chord, and the six scale patterns which overlay this chord form. We place this chord at the ninth fret and this makes the chord *A* major, and each scale is an *A* type scale.

CHROMATIC SCALE – KEY OF *A*

MAJOR SCALE – KEY OF *A*

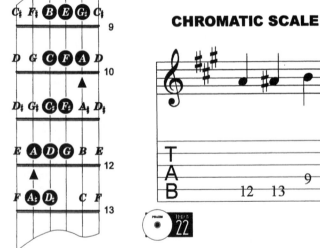

C FORM

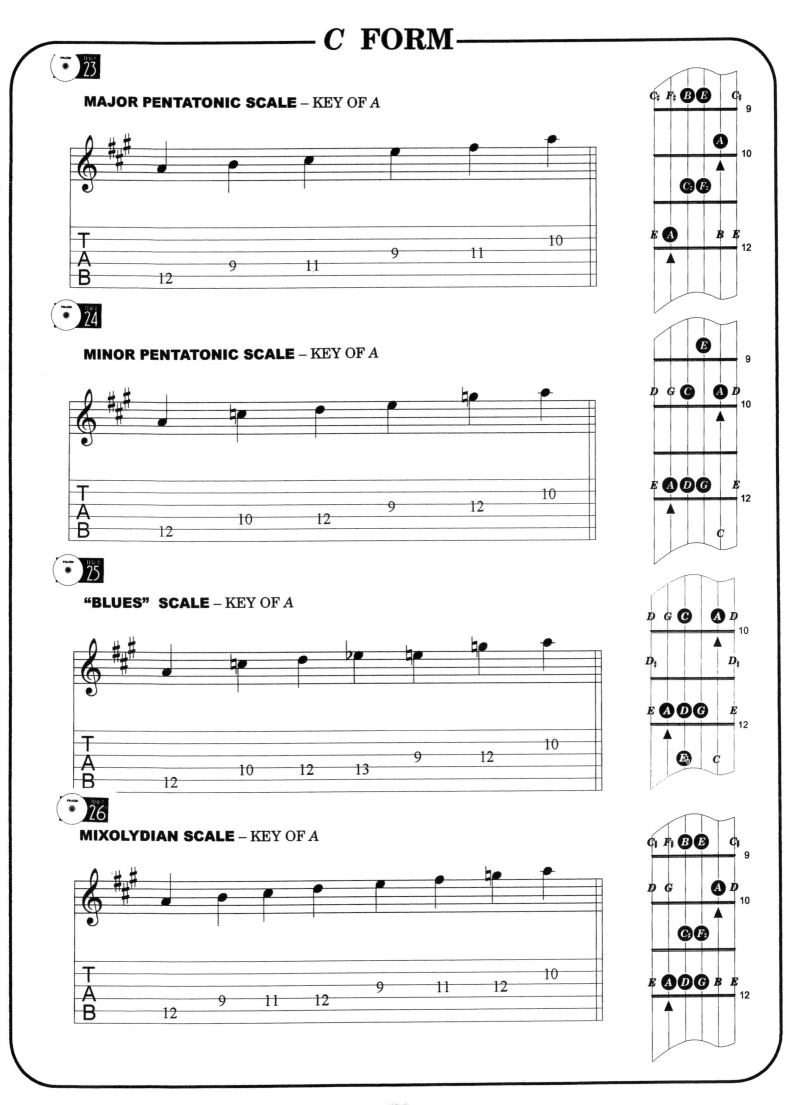

A Chord Scale Patterns

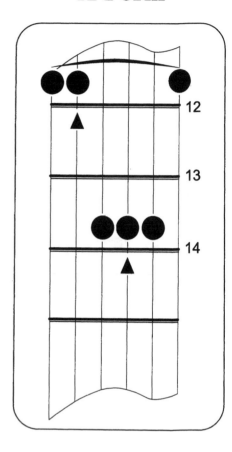

A Form

On the following page, we present the second pattern of the *C A G E D* system of scale patterns – the *A* chord form. We place the pattern at the twelfth fret. This makes the chord *A* major, and each scale is an *A* type scale.

Thoughts on Ear Training

Guitarists must develop a variety of skills that embody the essence of creating music *on the fly*. One of the most important requirements is the ability to hear changes in pitch, like chord changes, and the differences in pitch between scale tones.

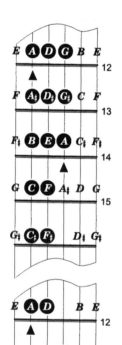

CHROMATIC SCALE – KEY OF *A*

MAJOR SCALE – KEY OF *A*

A FORM

MAJOR PENTATONIC SCALE – KEY OF A

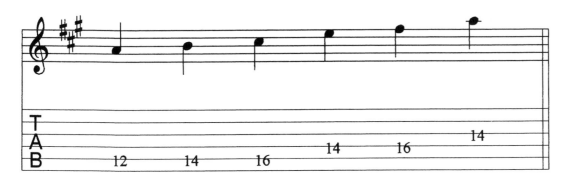
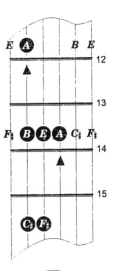

MINOR PENTATONIC SCALE – KEY OF A

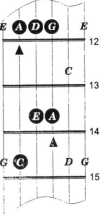

"BLUES" SCALE – KEY OF A

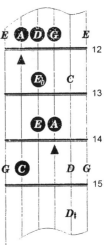

MIXOLYDIAN SCALE – KEY OF A

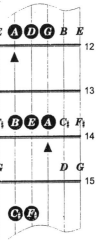

G Form

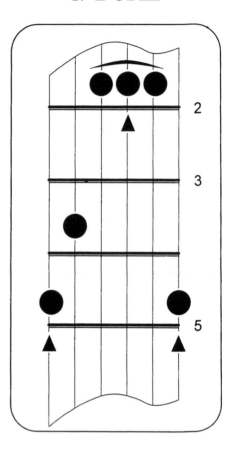

G Chord Scale Patterns

On the following page, we present the third pattern of the *C A G E D* system of scale patterns – the *G* chord form. We place this pattern at the second fret. This makes the chord *A* major, and each scale is an *A* type scale.

Advantages of the *C A G E D* System

There are several advantages of using the *C A G E D* system of scale management. First, these fingerings are designed to emphasize the root of the chord, or first note of the scale pattern. This feature helps you stay oriented when you improvise. Second, you have better visualization of the fretboard, because the scale pattern overlays the chord shape.

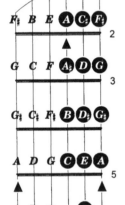

CHROMATIC SCALE – KEY OF *A*

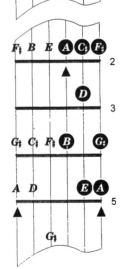

MAJOR SCALE – KEY OF *A*

G FORM

MAJOR PENTATONIC SCALE – KEY OF A

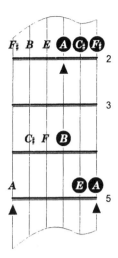

MINOR PENTATONIC SCALE – KEY OF A

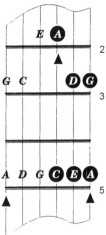

"BLUES" SCALE – KEY OF A

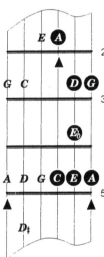

MIXOLYDIAN SCALE – KEY OF A

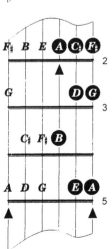

E Chord Scale Patterns

E Form

On the following page, we present the fourth pattern of the *C A G E D* system of scale patterns – the *E* chord form. We place this pattern at the fifth fret. This makes the chord *A* major, and each scale is an *A* type scale.

The Use of Multiple-Scale Patterns in Playing Great Solos

The blues is the focus of our studies, primarily because of the tonal structure of the minor pentatonic scale. But the blues' influence on other styles of music lends itself to several, if not all six, scale patterns in the *C A G E D* system. Great blues players move in and out of different scales to influence their individual style, or to enhance a particular passage in a song. Moving between the major and minor pentatonic scale is a common device used by Country and Blues players alike. Rockabilly phrases also encompass tones from both scales. Study the differences between the *major pentatonic* and the *minor pentatonic* scale, and notice how close these two scales are associated within the box position of each *C A G E D* pattern of scales.

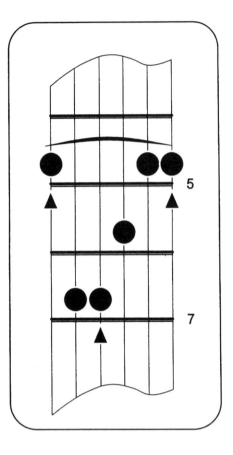

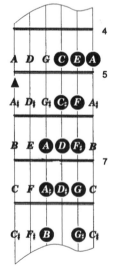

CHROMATIC SCALE – KEY OF *A*

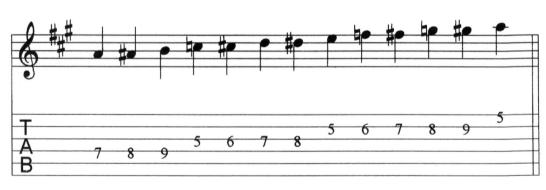

MAJOR SCALE – KEY OF *A*

A major scale
Key of A

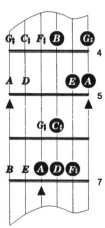

E FORM

MAJOR PENTATONIC SCALE – KEY OF *A*

MINOR PENTATONIC SCALE – KEY OF *A*

"BLUES" SCALE – KEY OF *A*

MIXOLYDIAN SCALE – KEY OF *A*

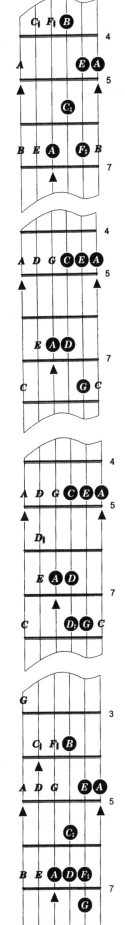

D Chord Scale Patterns

On the following page, we present the fifth pattern of the *C A G E D* system of scale patterns – the *D* chord, form five. We place this pattern at the seventh fret. This makes the chord *A* major, and each scale is an *A* type scale.

Getting the Most Out of Scale Practice

Learn each scale pattern by playing slowly with melodic feel. Let each tone ring. Pay attention to the fingering and develop the reach required in order to play each note cleanly. When comfortable with the finger pattern, experiment with simple phrases by varying the dynamics and timing. Play a relatively slow tempo and concentrate on phrases that capture the shuffle beat. Experiment with short three, or four note riffs, and use bends and pauses to create musical ideas. Also, try skipping notes of the scale. Get away from simply playing up an down the scale. Vary your picking technique by striking the strings with different degrees of pressure when picking notes.

D Form

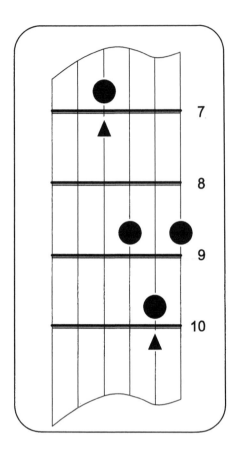

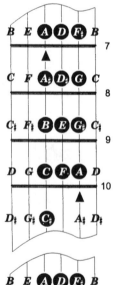

CHROMATIC SCALE – KEY OF *A*

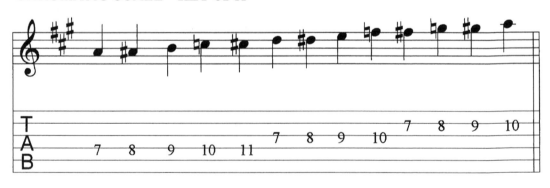

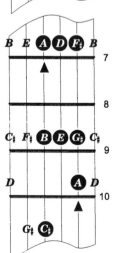

MAJOR SCALE – KEY OF *A*

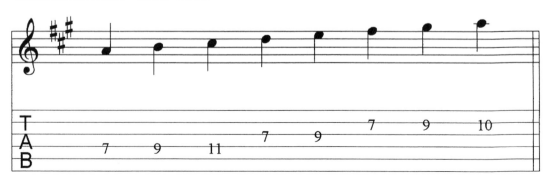

D FORM

MAJOR PENTATONIC SCALE – KEY OF *A*

MINOR PENTATONIC SCALE – KEY OF *A*

"BLUES" SCALE – KEY OF *A*

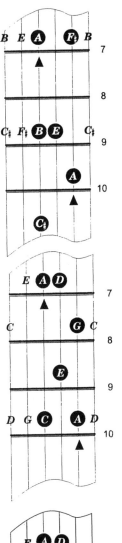

MIXOLYDIAN SCALE – KEY OF *A*

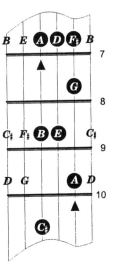

SCALES OVER CHORDS

How to improvise . . . and never play bad notes!

by WILBUR M. SAVIDGE
and RANDY LEE VRADENBURG

HOW TO PLAY
LEAD LINES OVER
CHORD PROGRESSIONS
AND NEVER PLAY BAD NOTES.
HOW TO CREATE AND USE INTERVALS,
SCALES, MODES AND ARPEGGIOS
IN ANY KEY.

WRITTEN IN NOTATION AND TABLATURE.
REVISED CD EDITION

P
PRAXIS

BS70297

PRAXIS MUSIC PUBLICATIONS, INC.

Section Four

BLUES EXPRESSION TOOLS

Bends-vibratos-slides

Hammer-ons

Double stops

Slides

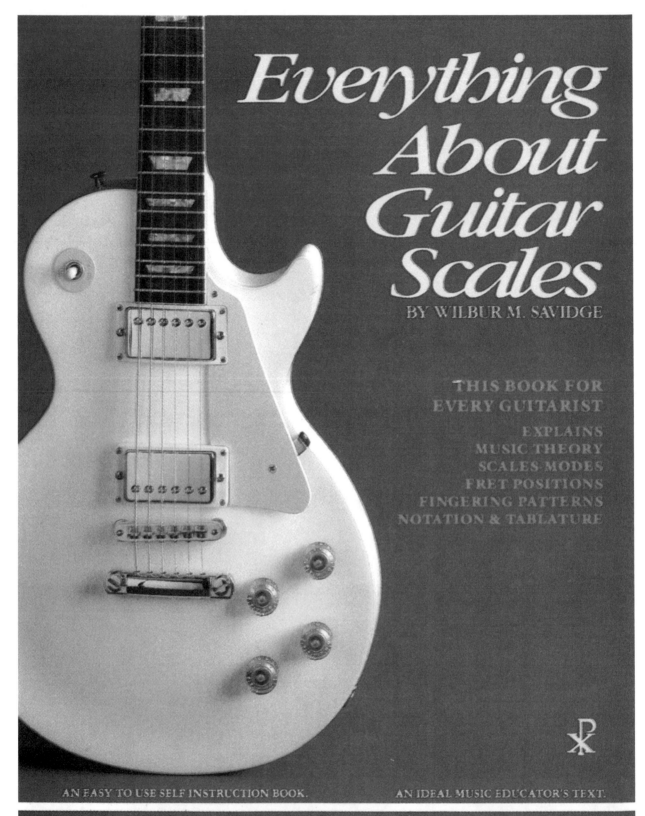

Everything About Guitar Scales

BY WILBUR M. SAVIDGE

THIS BOOK FOR
EVERY GUITARIST

EXPLAINS
MUSIC THEORY
SCALES-MODES
FRET POSITIONS
FINGERING PATTERNS
NOTATION & TABLATURE

AN EASY TO USE SELF INSTRUCTION BOOK.   AN IDEAL MUSIC EDUCATOR'S TEXT.

BS 70294   PRAXIS MUSIC PUBLICATIONS, INC.

EXPRESSION TOOLS

Playing blues requires more than a few choice notes to create a *"blues solo"*. You must be able to play with feeling! Listen to a great blues guitarist and you will hear this expression of honest emotion. This intensity of feeling is created by using *"expression tools"*. There are seven expression tools guitarists use in blues phrasing: 1) **String Bending**, 2) **Vibrato**, 3) **Slides**, 4) **Hammer-ons**, 5) **Pull-offs**, 6) **Rake**, 7) **Double Stops**.

String Bending

"String bending" is a way of playing more than one note without plucking the string a second time. By *"pushing"* the string, a fretted tone can be raised in pitch thus, creating a variety of additional tones. Bends may be only a subtle *"push"* of the string, a slight, often momentary increase in pitch of the note (a quarter tone or less), to a one fret increase in pitch (a half-step) and even a whole-step bend (a distance of two frets). A one or two fret bend is standard fare in blues playing, however many guitarists go much further and use what is called a *"wide bend"*, or *"over bend"* (a bend of three frets or more!). Great blues guitarists like Buddy Guy, Otis Rush and Albert King, have created entire riffs utilizing two and three step bends. In addition to the straightforward *"push"* bend, there is the *"pull down"* or *"reverse"* bend. This type of bend is most often used on the lower strings and is executed by pulling the string down to change the pitch. Regardless of the bend type, **the tone achieved by the bend must be either to a scale tone or a chord note.**

A string bend requires the physical ability to push the string far enough, and the auditory ability to know that the tone has been raised sufficiently in pitch to create the desired note. Each string on the guitar has its own physical dynamics that determines the amount of pressure required by the finger to push the string far enough to execute a proper bend. To add strength and support to the finger used to accomplish the bend, it should be supported by the other fingers. In this manner, the entire hand is involved in the bending process.

Bends

"Upward bend" is a bend created by pushing the string up, thus increasing the tension and raising a tones pitch. An upward bent note may be held (sustained), or cut short. To dampen the note, let the outside edge of the picking hand touch the string after the note is plucked This technique is called *"right hand blocking"*. The thumb of the picking hand is often employed in stopping the plucked string from vibrating. The string may also be dampened by bringing the pick up against the string. In standard notation, a grace note (a small eighth note) placed before the written note indicates the pitch of the note to be bent. The full size written note shows the actual pitch achieved by the bend.

Upward bends are marked with an *"upward"* curved arrow placed above the staff. The arrow begins above the grace not and curves up over the desired bent tone. A number placed above the arrow indicates how far to bend: The word *"full"* indicates a whole-step bend (two tones, two frets apart), the numeral 1/2 indicates a half-step bend (two tones, one fret apart), and the numeral 1/4 indicates a quarter-step bend.

In TAB, the first number placed on the line representing the string shows the correct fret upon which the finger should be placed to affect the bend. The next number is the fret the tone should be bent up to. A *"curved arrow"* is placed over the fret number of the tone to be bent. Above the arrow is a number indicating the correct bend to achieve the proper bent note. The number under the arrow is the fret number where the bent tone is located if it were plucked.

"Bend and release" is a note that is created by first striking the string, then pushing the string up, raising the tone's pitch and while keeping the pressure on the string, releasing the bend, thus allowing the sting to return to its normal position. This effect creates two uninterrupted notes. Bend and release notes are indicated by an arrow placed above the

staff that curves up from the first note and then returns to the second note. In TAB, a push and release note is represented by three fret numbers placed on the line representing the correct string. The first number is the *"pushed"* note. The second number is the fret of the correct pitch of the push note. The third number is the fret number of the *"release"* tone. The release bend is a note played after the string has already been pushed up to the desired note. Then, the bent tone is released, therefore lowering the fretted note. *Remember:* The string is only plucked once to achieve a *"push and release"* tone!

"Pre-bend" is a bending technique that functions in reverse of the regular bend. The pre-bend is created by pushing the string up to the desired first note *before* plucking the string. After the string is plucked, the bend is released, lowering the tone down to the correct note. In written notation, an arrow, shown as a vertical line, is placed above the note the string is pre-pushed up to. A curved arrow returns to the note the released tone creates. In TAB, the vertical line is placed above the fret number of the pushed note. The curved arrow returns to the next number which represents the fret placement of the pre-bent note.

"Microtonal Bend" is a bend that is less then one-half tone. It is a note that cannot be otherwise fretted for it falls between the frets. This type of bend is called a *"smear"* or quarter-tone bend.

Vibrato

"Vibrato" is perhaps the most difficult blues technique to develop. Yet, it is the most expressive musical effect associated with blues phrasing. Executed properly, the guitarist can produce a throbbing, shimmering sound which mimics the natural quiver or oscillation of the human voice. The tonal effect of the vibrato is created by a rapid *"push and release"* of the string. To create a *"finger"* vibrato, place the fretting hand loosely behind the neck with the thumb resting lightly on the outside edge. Strike the string firmly with the pick before beginning the vibrato. The wrist is bent in and out and the hand is shaken rapidly and evenly. The direction of the motion is similar to that of turning a door knob. The motion requires using the wrist and upper forearm muscles. The B. B. King *"wrist"* vibrato, often called a *"hummingbird vibrato"*, is created by a quick push and release using only the first finger. This type of vibrato requires a very rapid motion with only the finger in contact with the string. The thumb does not touch the back of the neck of the guitar. The faster the hand shakes the better the vibrato sounds.

Slides

"Slides" are indispensable in playing blues. They are simple, but always great sounding techniques. The slide is a way of picking the string and then playing two or more notes. The first note is fretted either above or below the target tone and is then plucked. While continuing to keep the finger firmly on the string, slide the finger along the string to the desired note. It is possible to slide into a new note from anywhere on the string while maintaining a continuous tone. The speed with which you play the slide is a matter of personal taste and should relate to the song you are playing. It is also a way the left hand can move smoothly from one position to another. In standard notation, and TAB, a slide is indicated by the letter "**s**" placed above a small angled line. Placed before a note it indicates an upward slide to a higher note. An angled line after a note indicates a slide downward to a lower note.

"Unison slide" is a device enabling the guitarist to play the same note on two strings. It is accomplished by playing a note on one string, and then sliding to the same note on an adjacent string. This technique creates a unique sound, and is an effective method for changing scale positions.

EXPRESSION TOOLS

Slur

"Slurs" In standard notation, slurs are indicated by a small curved line placed over two notes. This mark generally indicates either a *"pull-off"* or a *"hammer-on"*, two notes created while striking the string only one time.

Hammer-On (Ascending slur)

"Hammer-on", is a fingering technique by which a note is played by plucking the string with the pick and generating another note by striking the string sharply with a finger on another fret while continuing to keep the pressure on the original tone. The *"hammer"* technique creates a second tone. In standard notation, a hammer-on is indicated by a slur mark, a curved line placed over both notes. In TAB, the letter "H" is placed above a curved line to indicate the effected notes.

Pull-Off (Descending slur)

"Pull-off" is a technique that allows two notes to be played in succession on one string, while picking the string only once. To effect a pull-off, two notes must be fretted before the string is plucked. With both notes fretted, the string is struck soundly to generate the higher note. Then, the finger on the higher tone is pulled sharply off the string to allow the pitch to revert to the lower fretted note. In standard notation, a pull-off is indicated by a slur mark (a curved line placed over both notes). In TAB, and in standard notation, the letter "P" is placed over the group of effected notes. The hammer-on/pull-off is a great way to play *"triplets"* (three notes while picking the string only once!).

Rake

"Rake" is a term that is used to define an abrupt down-stroke across muted strings. It is a musical device that is used by guitarists to create a **"high point"** within a musical phrase. The rake is played with deadened strings and is used to support a clean tone. To play a rake, sweep the pick down across the top four strings with an aggressive down-stroke while the fingers of the left hand dampen the fourth, third and second strings. Let the note on the first string ring clear. As you stroke the strings with a downward movement of the pick, let the edge of the right hand also dampen the muted strings. It is this coordination between the right and left hand that creates the **"rake"**.

Double Stops

"Double stops" are two notes played simultaneously. When located on adjacent strings, the pick is used to play the notes. If the two notes are separated by more than one string, guitarists often use their pick and fingers. (This technique involves **"hybrid picking"** which is discussed in detail later in this book).

EXPRESSION TOOLS

Phrasing

The great blues player doesn't think in terms of scale patterns, or grouping notes by sound. Tonal patterns or shapes, are the bi-products of phrasing, musical ideas based on the speech patterns of people talking or singing. These blues guitarists sing every note they play because singing enables them to better control their rhythm and phrasing, it helps their solos *"breathe"*. Stevie Ray Vaughan and B. B. King are great examples of guitarists that *"sing"* what they play! *"Phrasing"* is the arrangement of notes into complete, or incomplete ideas. It is about the manipulation of the notes we play. It is like talking: We may play a note or group of notes harshly or softly, and we may also play them fast or slow. Phrasing is simply a way of honestly expressing ourselves through our instrument. In speech, we may connect a series of words into a complete statement, or we may leave a sentence open-ended by asking a question, which demands an answer or resolution by a follow up statement.

Like language, musical phrasing parallels speech patterns. If one musical sentence states a subject, we expect the following sentence to extend, answer, qualify, or clarify it.

Great blues players, in addition to utilizing scales, have developed the ability to create short riffs that incorporate interval skips (non-scale movement of tones) and pauses that punctuate and add color to a solo. They also have developed the ability to imitate the phrasing and tone quality of horn players. The need for horn players to breathe, establishes pauses that effect the player's solos.

Motifs

"Motifs" are a short series of notes that create a short melodic statement. A motif may be only two or three notes in length; however, a well constructed motif will become a recognizable part of the song.

Riffs

"Riffs" can be thought of as a complete, but short musical ideas. It is a repetitive melodic figure that is an integral part of the song. A riff is a series of notes played in a particular sequence that makes a musical statement that is interesting, coherent, and expresses emotion. A great riff often becomes the signature lick in a particular solo.

Fills

A *"fill"* is a short phrase similar to a riff. However, unlike a riff which is usually a practiced phrase, a fill is spontaneous. It is invented on the spot. A fill is often used to fill the breaks around vocal phrasing. It is also used to keep the music moving. A fill should lead the listener smoothly out of one melody statement into the next melodic statement.

Bending in Tune

Finding and maintaining proper pitch is the biggest problem a new blues guitarist will encounter when bending a note. Pitch accuracy requires knowing how far to push the string to achieve the desired pitch. But, what is the pitch we are trying to reach when pushing the string? What is the desired note we wish to create with the bend? Bent notes are either scale tones or chord tones. Ear training via experimentation is the only real solution.

It is important to understand the effect we wish to create when using bends. Some bends create only one note, others create two, or even three different notes. We begin our study of note bending with the "*upward*" half-step and whole-step bend. This type of bend is used to create one note. The string is plucked, then pushed up to the desired tone. The tone is stopped before finger pressure on the string is release. In this manner, the "*pushed*" tone is the desired note. To help develop this important aspect of blues playing, we will make references to the following terms:

Comparison tone – A "*comparison tone*" is a device utilized when practicing pitch bending and is used to develop pitch accuracy. It is a note sounded as a reference tone. Then, execute a bend up to the comparison note. A properly executed bend requires extensive ear training and wrist control. You must always be able to "*hear*" the correct pitch of the bent note.

Approach tone – An "*approach tone*" is the fretted note the finger is placed upon to begin an "upward" bend.

Target pitch – The "*target pitch*" is the desired tone we wish to acheive when implementing an "*upward*" bend. A half-step bend will create a target pitch (note) on the next higher fret. A whole-step bend, also called a "*full*" bend, will create a target pitch (note) two frets above the fretted note.

Reading Bends
in Notation and Tab

In standard notation, a bent pitch is written with a note placed on the staff indicating the pitch of the target zone. A grace note (a small note) placed to the left of the target note represents the pitch of the tone to be pushed. A curved arrow placed above the two notes indicates the bend. The word "*full*" indicates a whole-step bend. The fraction 1/2 placed above the arrow indicates a half-step bend.

In TAB, two numbers are used to indicate a bend. The first number is the fret upon which the finger is placed to activate the bend (the approach tone). The second number is the fret number where the target pitch is located.

EXPRESSION TOOLS

DEVELOPING THE 1/2 STEP BEND

A half-step bend raises the pitch of the fretted note a half tone, or the distance of one fret on the guitar fretboard.

ILLUSTRATION ONE (first string)

COMPARISON TONE: The "comparison tone" is the target note of the bend. In the first measure of Illustration One, we establish our comparison tone. The comparison tone in this example is the note C, and it is played at the eighth fret. To achieve the half-step bend, we fret the note B at the seventh fret with the third finger, then push up on the string until the pushed up note sounds the same as the comparison tone C.

APPROACH TONE: In the second measure, we play the two notes involved in this one fret bend. The "approach tone" is the note B.

TARGET TONE: In measure three, we play the approach tone (a B note), then push the string sufficiently to sound our "target tone" – C. (Note: The comparison tone and the target tone are the same.)

RIFF APPLICATION: Measure four and five incorporates a half-step bend into an abbreviated blues lick.

ILLUSTRATION TWO (second string)

We now move to the second string – B. The "comparison tone" is the note G, and is played at the eighth fret. Our approach tone is $F\#$ at the seventh fret. Bend up a half-step to reach the target tone, note G.

ILLUSTRATION THREE (third string)

In Illustration Three, we place the half-step bend on the third string – G. The "comparison tone" is the note Eb. The approach tone is D. We bend the approach tone up to the target tone Eb.

HALF-STEP BENDS

ILLUSTRATION ONE   FIRST STRING

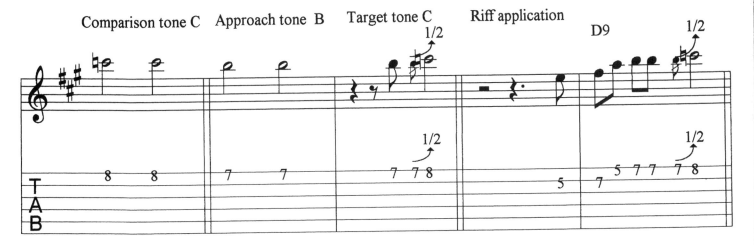

ILLUSTRATION TWO   SECOND STRING

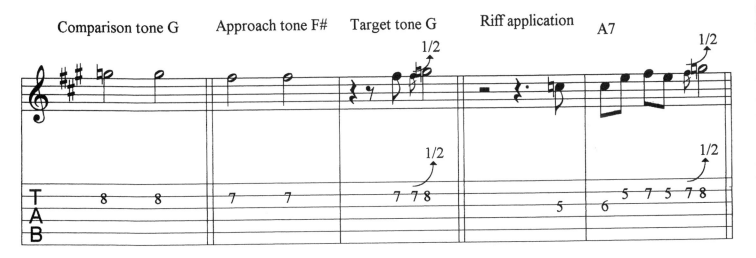

ILLUSTRATION THREE   THIRD STRING

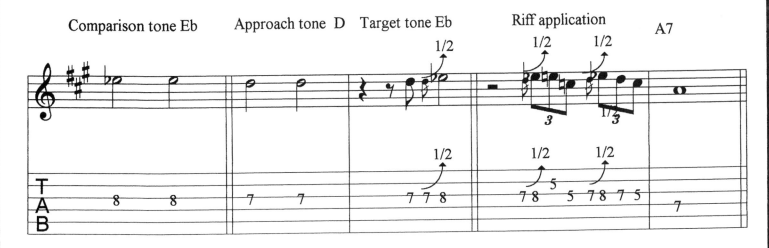

DEVELOPING THE
WHOLE-STEP "FULL" BEND

A whole-step (full) bend raises the pitch of the fretted note a full tone, or the distance of two frets on the guitar fretboard.

ILLUSTRATION ONE (first string)

COMPARISON TONE: In the first measure of Illustration One, we establish our "comparison tone". The comparison tone is the note C# and it is played at the ninth fret. To achieve the whole-step bend, a distance of two frets, also called a "full bend", we fret the note B at the seventh fret, a whole tone below our comparison tone, then push up on the string until the pushed note sounds the same as the comparison tone.

APPROACH TONE: In the second measure, we play the two notes involved in this one fret bend. The "approach tone" is the note *B*.

TARGET TONE: In the second measure, we play the two notes involved in this two fret bend. In the third measure, we play the *B* note, then push it up to *C#*. In measures four and five, we incorporate a whole-step bend in a two bar riff.

RIFF APPLICATION: Measures four and five incorporate a whole-step bend into an abbreviated blues lick.

ILLUSTRATION TWO (second string)

We now move to the second string – *B*. The "comparison tone" is the note *G#*, and is played at the ninth fret.

ILLUSTRATION THREE (third string)

In Illustration Three, we place the whole-step bend on the third string – *G*. The "comparison tone" is the note *E*.

WHOLE-STEP "FULL" BEND

ILLUSTRATION ONE
FIRST STRING

Comparison tone C#   Approach tone B   Target tone C#   Riff application

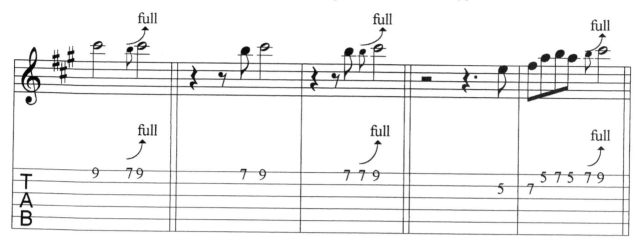

ILLUSTRATION TWO
SECOND STRING

Comparison tone G#   Approach tone F#   Target tone G#   Riff application

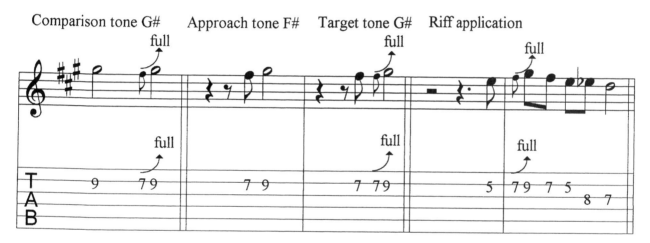

ILLUSTRATION THREE

THIRD STRING

Comparison tone E   Approach tone D   Target tone E   Riff application

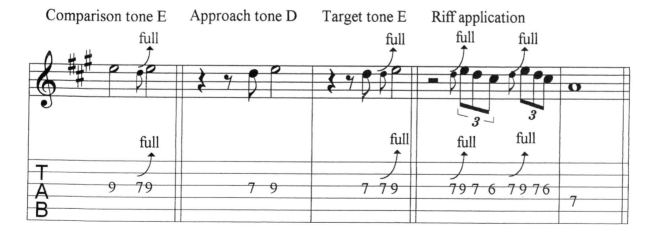

DEVELOPING THE
"BEND & RELEASE" BEND

Half-Step Bend & Release Bend

A "bend & release" creates two notes. First, the "push" tone (the target tone) created at the height of the bend; and second, the tone created after the bent tone is released. Either note of the bend and release bends may be a quarter note, half note, or a whole note in duration. In standard notation, a grace note places the finger on the correct tone to be "pushed", and the note following it is the note created by the push. The next note indicates the release note. An upward pointing arrow indicates the upward bend, and the downward curving arrow indicates the release bend. In TAB, it requires three fret numbers to indicate a push and release bend. The first number marks the fret placement of the note to be pushed. This is the note plucked. The second number indicates the fret (pitch) location of the "bent" tone. The third number represents the fret placement of the release tone. (The middle number is not plucked). In the first measure of each exercise, we place the three notes utilized when creating a bend and release. In measure two and three, we incorporate a bend and release into a blues riff.

> NOTE: As with all examples in this book, be sure to practice these exercises against the shuffle rhythm!

ILLUSTRATION ONE
HALF-STEP BEND & RELEASE BEND

In the first measure of Illustration One, we place the three notes utilized in creating a half-step bend & release bend on the first string. In the second measure, the note B (first string, seventh fret) is sounded. Then, while pressure is maintained on the string, the string is pushed up a half-step to create the pitch of the desired note (in this example, the C natural). Then, while the pressure on the string is maintained, the bend is released, lowering the tone to sound the B note. An example is played on the first three strings to give you the experience of creating a half-step bend & release on different strings.

ILLUSTRATION TWO
WHOLE-STEP BEND & RELEASE

In the first measure of Illustration Two, we place the three notes utilized in creating a whole-step bend & release bend on the second string. In the second measure, the note B (second string, seventh fret) is sounded. Then, while pressure is maintained on the string, the string is pushed up a whole-step to create the pitch of the desired note (in this example, the C sharp). Then, while the pressure on the string is maintained, the bend is released, thus lowering the tone to sound the B note. An example is played on the first three strings to give you the experience of creating a whole-step bend & release on different strings.

BEND & RELEASE BEND

DEVELOPING THE
"PRE-BEND & RELEASE" BEND

The "pre-bend & release" is an effective statement bending technique frequently used by blues guitarists. To execute a pre-bend & release bend, the string is bent to the proper pitch before the note is plucked. The bent string is struck and then released, thus creating a descending tone. A "pre-bent" note must be a scale tone or chord tone and must be "released" to a scale tone or chord tone.

In standard notation, a grace note indicates the fret location that the finger is placed on to execute the upward push. A vertical line is placed over the grace note to indicate the upward push (the string is not struck before the upward bend). A curved line then descends to the target tone. This is the note that is sounded at the height of the bend and is the descending pitch created by the release of the pre-bend. In TAB, a vertical line is placed over the fret number of the tone pre-pushed. A curved line then descends to the fret number of the target tone.

ILLUSTRATION ONE
HALF-STEP PRE-BEND & RELEASE

To execute the half-step pre-bend & release as shown in Illustration One, place your third finger on the seventh fret, first string – then push the string up a half-step (one fret). Pick the string sounding the tone, and release the bend. This will create a descending tone (*C* natural to *B* natural).

ILLUSTRATION TWO
WHOLE-STEP PRE-BEND & RELEASE

To execute the whole-step pre-bend & release as shown in Illustration Two, place your third finger on the seventh fret – then push the string up a whole-step (two frets). Pick the string sounding the tone, and release the bend. This will create a descending tone (*C#* natural to *B* natural).

"MAKIN' MUSIC"

Crank up the pre-bend & release . . . *and get with it!*

PRE-BEND & RELEASE

ILLUSTRATION ONE

HALF-STEP PRE-BEND & RELEASE

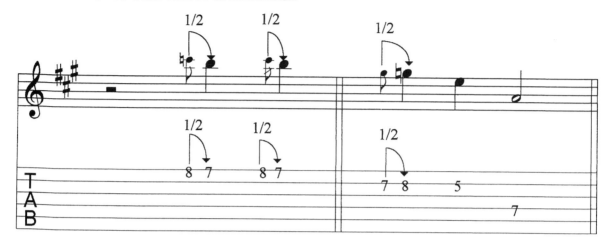

ILLUSTRATION TWO

WHOLE-STEP "FULL" PRE-BEND & RELEASE

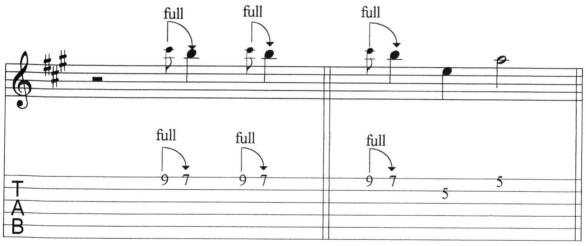

MAKIN' MUSIC

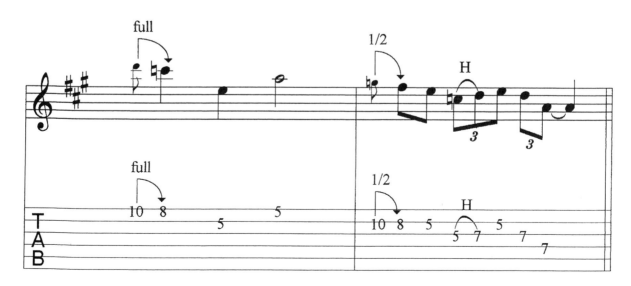

EXPRESSION TOOLS

HAMMER-ON

ILLUSTRATION ONE
HALF-STEP HAMMER-ON

In the first measure, we indicate the two notes to be sounded with the half-step hammer-on. In measure two, we show how this technique is noted. Fret the note *C* with your first finger. Then, strike the string and "hammer" your second finger on the next fret to create a half-step hammer-on. In measure three, we incorporate a half-step hammer-on into a blues riff.

LLUSTRATION TWO
WHOLE-STEP HAMMER-ON

In the first measure, we indicate the two notes to be sounded with the whole-step hammer-on (a distance of two frets). In measure two, we show how this whole-step hammer-on is noted. Fret the note *C* (third string, fifth fret) with your first finger. Then strike the string and "hammer" your third finger on the seventh fret to create a whole-step hammer-on. In measures three and four, we incorporate a whole-step hammer-on in a blues riff which resolves on the note *A* (the tonic note of the *A7* chord).

LLUSTRATION THREE
STEP AND A HALF HAMMER-ON

In the first measure, we indicate the two notes to be sounded playing a step and a half hammer-on (a distance of three frets). In measure two, we show this three fret hammer-on. Fret the note *E* (second string, fifth fret) with your first finger. Strike the string and "hammer" your third finger on the eighth fret. In measures three and four, we incorporate a step and a half hammer-on in a blues riff, which resolves on the note *A* (the tonic note of the *A7* chord).

HAMMER-ONS

ILLUSTRATION ONE

HALF-STEP HAMMER-ONS

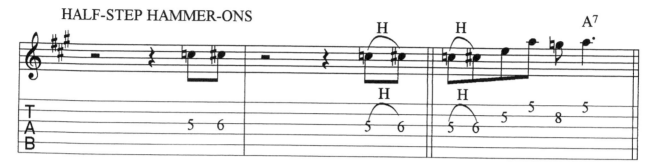

ILLUSTRATION TWO

WHOLE-STEP HAMMER-ONS

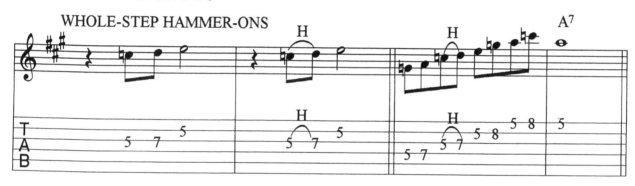

ILLUSTRTION THREE

ONE AND HALF STEP HAMMER-ONS

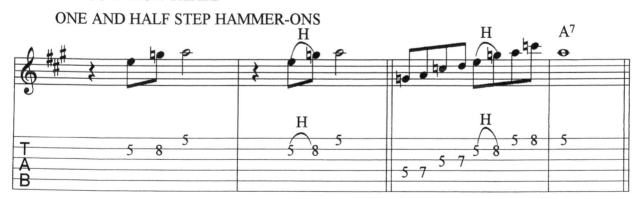

PULL-OFF

ILLUSTRATION ONE
HALF-STEP PULL-OFF

In the first measure, we indicate the two notes we use to execute a half-step pull-off (notes Eb and D, one fret apart on the fretboard). In the second measure, we use these two notes to play a half-step pull-off. Place your first finger on the seventh fret and your second finger on the eighth fret. Strike the string, sounding the eighth fret note – then pull your second finger off the string, allowing the pitch of the string to sound at the seventh fret. Executed properly, you will have created two notes of different pitch while striking the string only once.

> NOTE: Practice these excesses against a slow shuffle!

ILLUSTRATION TWO
WHOLE-STEP PULL-OFF

In the first measure we indicate the two notes we use to execute a whole-step pull-off. Notes B and A are two frets apart on the fretboard. In the second measure, we use these two notes to play a whole-step pull-off. Place your first finger on the fifth fret and your third finger on the seventh fret. Strike the string, sounding the seventh fret note – then pull your third finger off the string. This will allow the pitch of the string to sound at the fifth fret. Executed properly, you will have created two notes of different pitch while striking the string only once.

ILLUSTRATION THREE
ONE AND A HALF-STEP PULL-OFF

In the first measure we indicate the two notes we use to execute a one and a half-step pull-off. Notes C and A are three frets apart on the fretboard. In the second measure, we use these two notes to play a one and a half-step pull-off. Place your first finger on the fifth fret and your third finger on the eighth fret. Strike the string, sounding the eighth fret note – then pull your third finger off the string. This will allow the pitch of the string to sound at the fifth fret Executed properly, you will have created two notes of different pitch while striking the string only once.

ILLUSTRATION FOUR
DOUBLE PULL-OFF

In the first measure we indicate the three notes we use to execute a double pull-off – notes C, B and A. In the second measure, we use these three notes to play a double pull-off. Place your first finger on the note A, fifth fret and your third finger on the note B, seventh fret, and your fourth finger on the note C, eighth fret. Strike the first string, sounding the C note, then pull the fourth finger off the string sounding the B note, seventh fret, then pull the third finger off the seventh fret, sounding the note A, fifth fret. Executed properly, you will have played three notes of different pitch while striking the string only once. These three notes are "triplets". *NOTE*: These three notes should be played fairly rapidly in order to hear the double pull-off effect.

PULL OFF

HALF-STEP PULL-OFF

ILLUSTRATION ONE

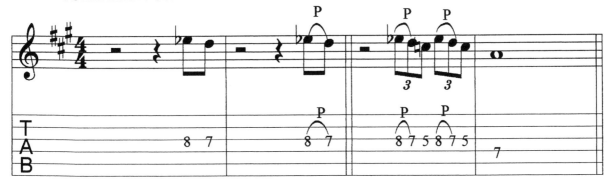

ILLUSTRATION TWO

WHOLE-STEP PULL OFF

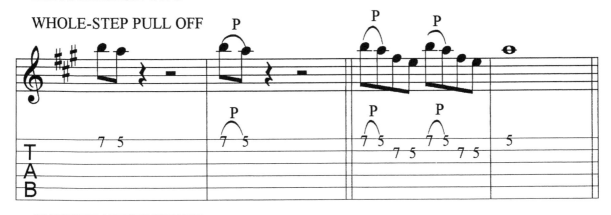

ILLUSTRATION THREE
ONE AND HALF-STEP PULL
OFF

ILLUSTRATION FOUR

DOUBLE PULL OFF

EXPRESSION TOOLS

Slides

ILLUSTRATION ONE

SLIDES

A slide may move either up or down the fretboard. When making a slide, pick the first note and while keeping pressure on the string, slide your finger to the next note. This will create a continuous sound from the first tone to the second tone. in written notation and TAB, a slant line is used to indicate a slide. Use the second finger to perform this slide.

HALF-STEP SLIDES

In the first measure, we indicate the two notes to be played to execute a half-step slide. In the second measure, we play a half-step slide. In measure three, we incorporate a half-step slide in a blues riff. Use the second finger to perform this slide.

ILLUSTRATION TWO

WHOLE-STEP SLIDE

In the first measure, we indicate the two notes to be sounded with the whole-step slide. In the second measure, we play a whole-step slide. In measure three, we incorporate a whole-step slide in a blues riff. Use the third finger to execute this slide.

ILLUSTRATION THREE

UNISON SLIDE

The master of blues phrasing, B.B. King, may not have invented the **unison slide**, but it appears countless times in his signature solos. Executed properly, it is an ear catching expressing tool sure to add interest to your blues phrasing. A unison slide is performed by playing a note on one string and sliding to the same note on an adjacent string. Playing a note on one string and then sliding to the same note on another string, does execute a unison slide. However, it sounds rather bland. A great embellishment is to slide into the first note, and then slide up to the same note on the adjacent string. This adds a little feeling to the movement! Better yet, make the first note an eighth note, and make the second note a half note. Apply lots of vibrato and you can make a unison slide really sing. A short riff leading up to the first slide tone will make it all sound even better. Use the third finger to perform this slide.

SLIDES

ILLUSTRATION ONE
HALF-STEP SLIDE   UP-DOWN

ILLUSTRATION TWO
WHOLE-STEP SLIDE

ILLUSTRATION THREE
UNISON SLIDE

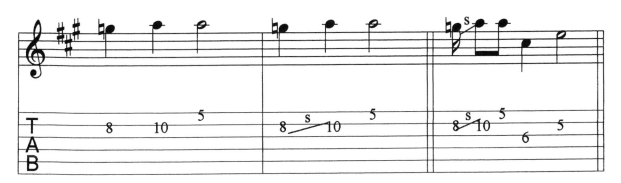

MAKIN' MUSIC

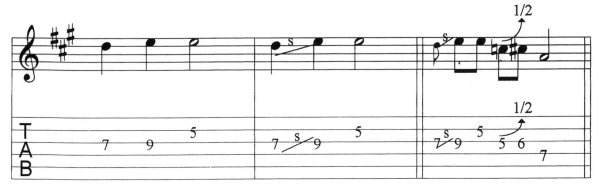

DOUBLE STOPS

DOUBLE STOPS

A "double stop" is a term applied to the playing of two notes at the same time. On the guitar, this would be two notes, each note on a different string, played simultaneously. When two or more notes are sounded together, rules of harmony must be applied so the effect will be melodic. The most common rule of harmony applied to double stops is the application of "thirds" (two notes a third interval apart). "Sixths" are also popular in playing double stops. Double stops may be played with a pick, or by using a combination of pick and fingers, called hybrid picking.

ILLUSTRATION ONE

In measure one, we have written a four note phrase using double stops. The fingering of double stops is most important. For the first double stops, use the first and second fingers. For the second double stops, use the first finger as a barr. For the third set of notes, use your second and third fingers. For the second set of double stops, use the first finger as a barr. For the fourth set of double stops, again, barr with the first finger. In measure two and three, we have written double stops as a blue phrase.

Playing tip: Practice this exercise until you can move smoothly through the entire phrase.

ILLUSTRATION TWO
DOUBLE STOP SLIDES

In this exercise, we incorporate double stops with slides, an effective blues device. Form the double stop with the first and second fingers, so the third finger may play the A note on the fourth string.

DOUBLE STOP SLIDES

ILLUSTRATION ONE
DOUBLE STOPS

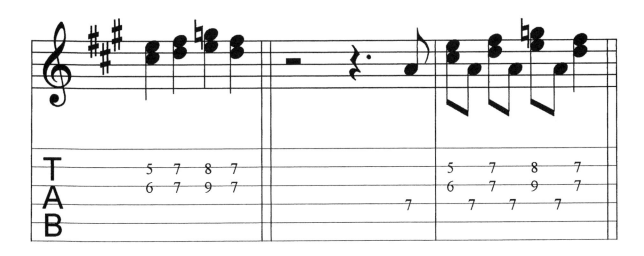

ILLUSTRATION TWO
DOUBLE STOP SLIDES

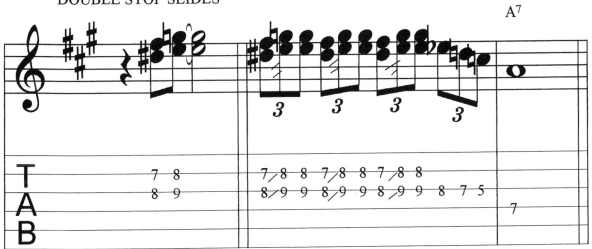

IMPLEMENTATION OF EXPRESSION TOOLS

Now we will experiment with the usage of expression tools, the whole-step bend, half-step bend, hammer-ons, pull-offs, and slides. As you develop your blues skills, you will come to realize how few notes are required to play the blues. One set group of notes are used repetitive in the four examples on the following page. By changing the type of expression tool applied to them, we change the effect of the riff.

ILLUSTRATION ONE
WHOLE-STEP BEND

The riff begins on the second beat of the first measure with a set of triplets.

ILLUSTRATION TWO
HALF-STEP BEND

In this example, we play the same group of notes and with the same rhythmic phrasing. However, we change the feel of the riff by changing the type of expression tool used.

ILLUSTRATION THREE
WHOLE-STEP HAMMER-ON

A riff may be altered by implementing expression tools on different beats and applied to different notes in the riff.

ILLUSTRATION FOUR
SLIDES

In this example, we significantly alter the riff by placing the note *A* on the second string, and implement a slide to make the transition . . . *a neat trick used by blues guitarists.*

IMPLEMENTATION OF EXPRESSION TOOLS

ILLUSTRATION ONE – WHOLE STEP BEND

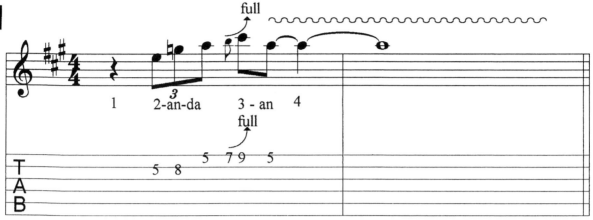

ILLUSTRATION TWO – HALF-STEP HAMMER-ONS
Pull-Off (Fingers 3-4)

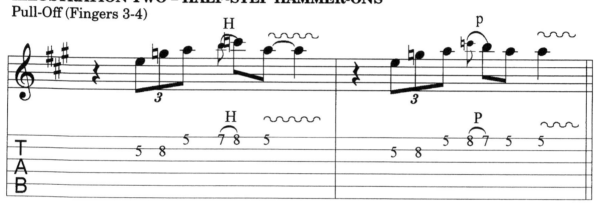

ILLUSTRATION THREE – WHOLE-STEP HAMMER-ONS
Pull-Off (Fingers 1-4)

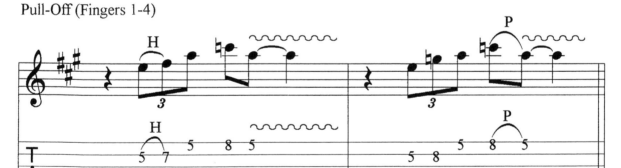

ILLUSTRATION FOUR – SLIDES
SLIDES

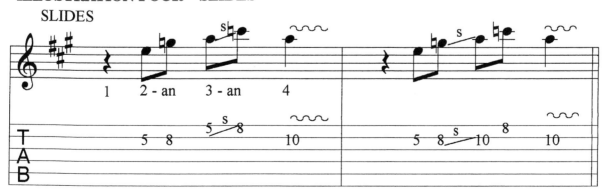

SOMETHING TO THINK ABOUT

BENDING TO CHORD TONES

Do you know your chord triads? You know, those three and four scale tone groups that form specific chords. Do you know the name of the notes on each string, the six chromatic scales that the guitar fretboard represents? Something to think about when bending notes. In the following examples we have laid out a blueprint of string bending chord tones found on the first and second string in the key of *A*. They are associated with the *A* pentatonic scaled played at the fifth fret.

In order to make your riffs sizzle, it is important to emphasize chord tones and bent notes will allow you to hit notes that will do just that. Bending up to a chord tone is thehallmark of great blues players.

In example one, we present the notes on the first string beginning at the fifth fret. By utilizing a half-step bend, a full step bend, and step and a half bend, it is possible to bend to a note found within each of the ryhtm chords – *A7, D7, E7*. Place your third finger on the seventh fret, the note is *B*. This note is the third of *E7*. A half-step bend will produce *C* natural, the flat seventh of *D7*. A full step bend will create *C#*, the third of *A7*. A step and half bend will produce the note *D*, the tonic (1) note of *D7*, and the flat seventh of *E7*.

In example two, we present the notes found on the second string beginning at the fifth fret. Place your finger on the fifth fret, this produces the note *E*, the tonic (1) of *E7* and the fifth of *A7*.Fret the seventh fret with your third finger, this produces the note *F#*. *F#* is the third of *D7*. A half-step bend with your third finger will produce *G* natural, the flat seventh of *A7*. A full-step bend produces the note *G#*, the third of *E7*.

Experiment with this concept, it's not really understood by all that many amateur players.

Something to think about.

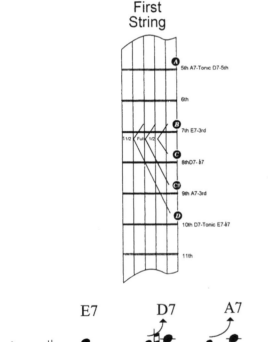

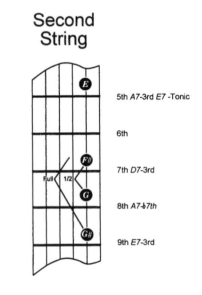

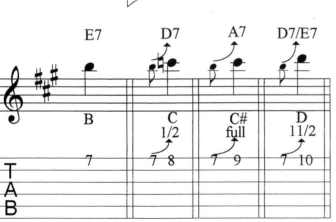

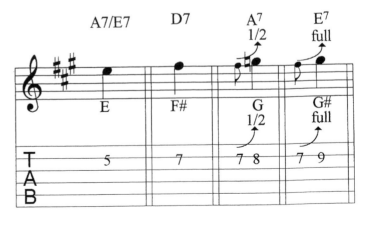

RIFF
CONSTRUCTION

Minor pentatonic scale

Riff alternation

Study in blues phrasing

The blues scale

Chord tone resolution

I-IV-V chord tones

I-IV chord change

Major third-Dominant seventh tones

V-IV chord change

SOMETHING TO THINK ABOUT

Playing By Ear

Do you listen to the notes you play? Have you developed an 'ear' for pitch function? One of the most important requirements of improvisation is the ability to hear how notes lead. Play two scale notes in consecutive order, then ask yourself what are the movement tendencies of the second note? Does it want to continue to rise? Fall back to the Tonic note of the scale? Or, does it remain neutral. Continue adding notes to the sequence and ask the same questions. Vary the interval between notes and see how they effect the stability or instability of a note.

Develop a riff that ends on a chord tone. Then, strum the chord and listen to the effect. Play the same riff over all three chords of the key in which you are playing and experiment by pausing on individual chord tones – do you like what you have played. Remember that there are many different ways of arriving at the same destination. Vary the riff by using expression tools.

Test your abilities. Play a blues scale and hum each note. Then hum the scale, stop on a note, and then play that note on the guitar. Hum a riff and see if you can play it accurately!

You cannot play interesting music if you have nothing going on in your head. Empty head – empty music. **Something to think about.**

RIFF CONSTRUCTION

Blues Study – First Riffs

From your experience playing blues scales, you will have noticed that nearly all the pentatonic notes sound good with all the chords in the blues chord progression. But, playing notes in no particular sequence becomes rather dull after awhile. A riff must make sense. It must be focused on a short series of notes that, in themselves, make a complete statement that is pleasant to the ear.

There are no definitive rules when creating blues riffs. However, there are a number of ideas that work better than others, such as short riffs, which are easier to develop than long ones. In order to add structure to a riff, resolve a chord tone; the root, third, fifth. When playing over a dominant chord, end on the flat seventh. Begin a riff on a chord tone and end the riff with a chord tone, in between, play scale notes with lots of interval skips. A riff, once developed, may be repeated in time, played backward, upside down, elongated, condensed or connected in series to develop a melodic phrase. The use of expression techniques such as the bend and vibrato add distinctive flair to a riff. The rhythm and dynamics of the notes used to play a riff may be changed. Quarter notes may be played as eighths, and the intervals between notes may be changed.

In this section, *Riff Construction*, we will explore these techniques, their creation, application, and provide insight into all aspects of creating blues riffs.

THE BLUES "BOX"

When asked to play a blues solo over the I-IV-V blues progression, nine out of ten times, the guitarist will blaze forth with riffs and licks played within a fixed position. The most common blues key is the key of *A*, played at the fifth fret. All the notes required are within this fixed position which we call a "box" position. Chord tones, scale tones, expression tones – all the tools required to play the blues, lie magically under the guitarist's fingers! It is this box position that we will use in our studies of how to play the blues.

RIFF CONSTRUCTION

Creating a One Bar Riff

We begin our study into the art of riff construction by creating riffs in the key of *A*. We use the *A* minor pentatonic scale, which is played from the *E* chord form scale pattern of the *CAGED* system. This places the "box" pattern at the fifth fret and it is one of the most common fingering patterns used by blues guitarists.

ILLUSTRATION ONE

Illustration One shows the *A* minor pentatonic scale played in the fifth position (fifth fret, first finger).

ILLUSTRATION TWO

In Illustration Two, we create a basic riff. It is a two bar riff written in 4/4 time and is played with quarter notes – a slow, methodical sequence. It is a simple riff with just enough notes to make a musical statement, and will introduce you to counting time and playing a minor pentatonic scale. This riff begins with a quarter note rest on the first beat. The first note of the riff begins on the second beat.

ILLUSTRATION THREE

Illustration Three is an example of how an original statement may be repeated, but altered to create a new riff by simply changing the rhythmic structure. In this example, we have changed the melodic figure by implementing triplets on the second beat and playing eighth notes on the third beat. Because we have changed the time value of the notes, figure three becomes a one bar riff. The last note of the riff is an eighth note played on the upbeat between the third and fourth beats. This is a "tied" note, and sustains through the fourth beat, a tied quarter note, which in turn, is tied to a whole note in the same measure. This riff is built with only four notes of the minor pentatonic scale and demonstrates how simplicity can be a valuable improvisational resource.

ILLUSTRATION FOUR

In Illustration Four, we have added "expression" with the use of the bend and a vibrato. On the third beat, we utilize a half step bend. We bend the note *B*, seventh fret, up a half step to create the *C* natural tone which would be created by fretting the eighth fret. We have not altered the rhythmic structure of the measure. A vibrato is played on the last note of the riff.

> **PLAYING TIP:** It is important to "feel" the shuffle beat.
> Count the rhythm before you play the riff.

A POSITIVE TOUGHT: Rethinking Illustrations 1-2-3-4

Experiment with these riffs. Notice how the use of the bend and vibrato make a series of notes sound "bluesy". These are the art forms you must master in order be a blues guitarist. NOTE: It is important to practice these excercises against the shuffle beat. Master the fingering patterns and then work to develop the shuffle feel. Also, listen to the great blues men and copy their riffs.

CREATING A ONE BAR RIFF

ILLUSTRATION ONE

FIFTH POSITION

ILLUSTRATION TWO

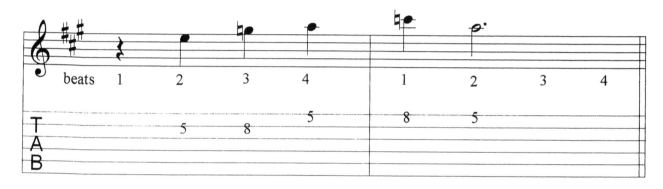

ILLUSTRATION THREE

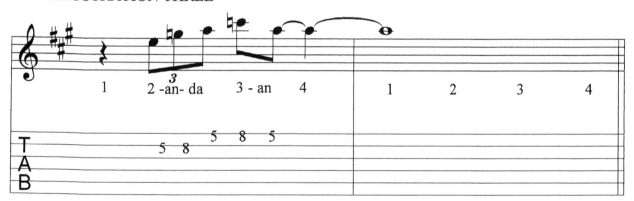

ILLUSTRATION FOUR

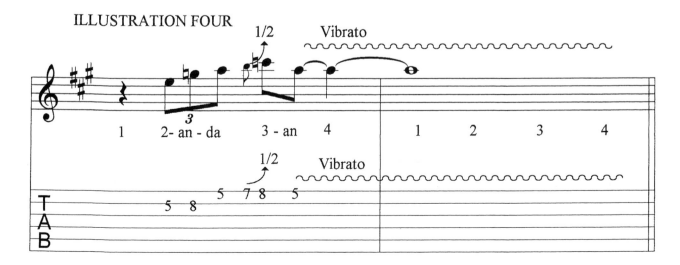

Riff Alteration

Once you learn to think in terms of "riff alteration", you will have acquired one of the real secrets of creating new and original blues riffs. Instead of meandering through the scale patterns searching for new note combinations to add excitement to your solos, look inward. Examine what you have already created – find new ways of playing the notes that comprise your current favorite riffs. Changing the time values of notes, utilizing different expression tools, and playing notes in a different sequence, and skipping strings, are common methods blues guitarists use to keep their solos fresh.

ILLUSTRATION ONE

Illustration One presents a simple one bar riff played across three strings. We incorporate a half-step bend.

ILLUSTRATION TWO

In Illustration Two, we utilize the same notes; however, we incorporate hammer-ons and a half-step bend.

ILLUSTRATION THREE

In Illustration Three, we alter the timing by using a triplet and a half-step pull-off.

ILLUSTRATION FOUR

In Illustration Four, we alter the riff by using triplets, a hammer-on and a pull-off.

RIFF ALTERATION

ILLUSTRATION ONE

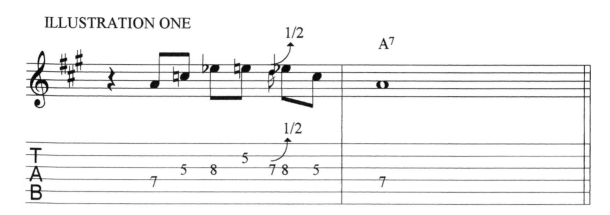

ILLUSTRATION TWO

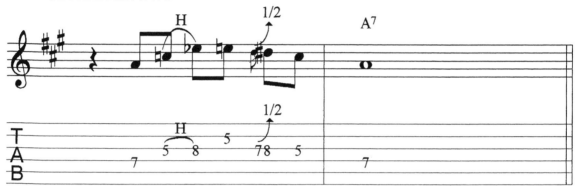

ILLUSTRATION THREE

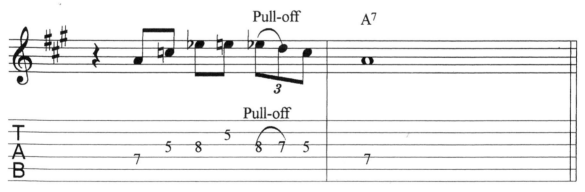

ILLUSTRATION FOUR

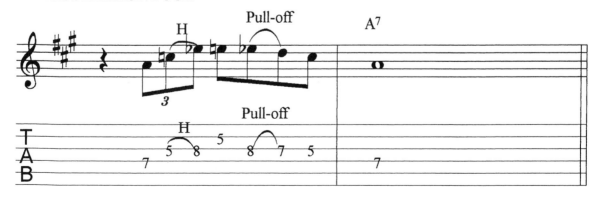

Hard Tone

ILLUSTRATION ONE

In this example, we explore the use of a slide, a half-step bend, a whole-step bend, and a vibrato. We also introduce a commonly used, but seldom explained expression device – a "hard tone". To execute a hard tone, pick the string with more force than normal. A hard tone makes a statement, an accent that calls your ear to that particular note. We use a > mark placed above the effected note to indicate a hard tone.

ILLUSTRATION TWO

Illustration Two is a variation on the first measure of the above exercise. It incorporates a hammer-on and pull-off. To properly execute the technique, fret the note A (fifth fret) with your first finger. Then, quickly pull the third finger off the string with sufficient force to sound the fifth fret note.

ILLUSTRATION THREE

Illustration Three wraps up this exercise in hard tones. The third measure ends on the root note of the I chord, A7. By ending on the root note, we bring resolution to the riff.

A POSITIVE THOUGHT: Rethinking III. 1-2-3

It is not the notes that make a blues riff. What counts is how they are used! This must include the subtleties of phrasing, timing, rhythm, dynamics, bends, vibrato, hammer-ons, pull-off, and other embellishments. In order to improvise the blues, you must learn how to take a few notes and make something happen! It's that simple. That is the magic of creating music spontaneously. Play a group of notes that harmonize the chord. Tinker with the subtleties, and suddenly – you are playing blues. Alter the timing, the dynamics; change the time value of the notes; and use the vibrato on different notes. Keep everything in meter, and play each measure in four beats. Experiment, experiment and experiment again with all these aspects of blues phrasing. This is the most fundamental lesson you will learn from this book!

PLAYING TIP: String bending requires accuracy to achieve the proper bent tone. When practicing, double check each bend (comparison technique) and make sure you are bending to the indicated pitch. String bending requires finger, hand and wrist strength. Practice each type of bend at various positions on the guitar neck. "Practice builds muscles!"

ALTERING RIFFS WITH EXPRESSION TOOLS

HARD TONES

ILLUSTRATION ONE

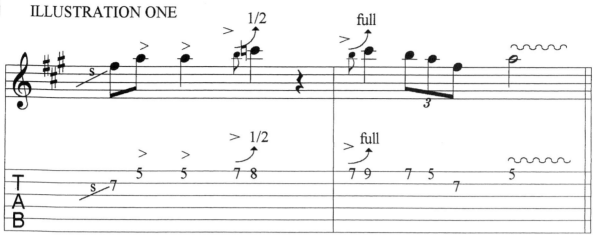

ILLUSTRATION TWO

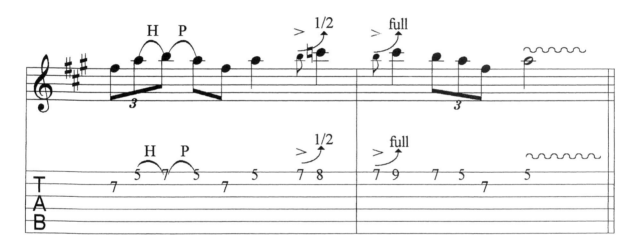

ILLUSTRATION THREE

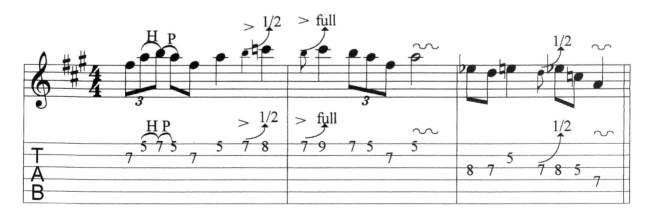

125

Hard One

In order to play the blues, we must be able to "feel" the type of rhythmic beat that is being used in the song. The blues guitarist must also be able to feel where the first beat of the measure begins. It is the blues soloist's responsibility to telegraph to the band and the listener, where the first beat of each measure begins. This first beat is referred to as the "solid one" or "hard" beat. To accent the beat, the first beat is often played with a "hard tone". Feeling where the first beat of the measure begins has a settling effect on the band and listener.

Pick-up notes from the previous measure are often used in blues solo to again, telegraph to the band and listener that the first beat is about to happen. Pick-up notes – eighth note triplets, or a signal eighth note are the most common rhythmic figure used by blues players. Any type of expression tool, including the "hard tone", may also be used in conjunction with the note value played, but the note values must match with the type of rhythm over which the solo is being performed. Since most blues rhythm patterns are shuffle rhythms, or a division of three, the triplet figure is a common pick-up device. They are played on the fourth beat of the previous measure to establish the "solid one". Triplets are perfect to set the band and the listener up for the solid one, and the hard tone accent.

HARD ONE

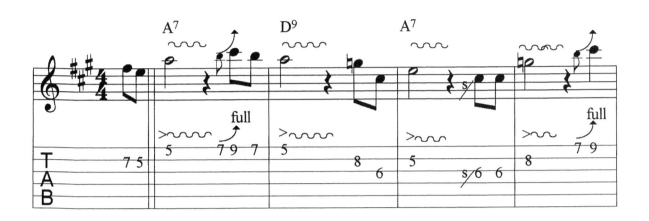

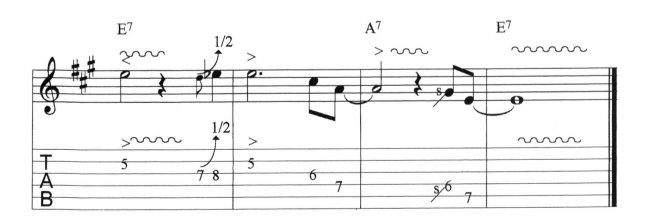

Triplet Study

Triplets, three notes of equal value played within the span of one beat, are an integral part of blues phrasing. Triplets are often played on the fourth beat of a measure to lead the phrase into the first beat of the following measure. Triplets often occur across strings and require practice in order to play them cleanly.

ILLUSTRATION ONE

Illustration one, we experiment with triplets used as a riff played on over the I-IV-V progression. The fingering is tricky and may require practice Be sure to use the fourth finger to play the notes that appear on the eighth fret (fifth position).

ILLUSRTATION TWO

Illustration two is continuation of our triplet study.

ILLUSTRATION THREE

Illustration Three includes a combination of hammer-ons, pull-offs, and slides. Note the position shift in measure three. This can be a taxing combination of expression tools and we suggest that you practice this example until you can perform it with ease.

TRIPLET STUDY

RIFF CONSTRUCTION
Study in Phrasing

QUARTER TONE BEND

A "quarter tone" bend is called a "smear" or small bend, and is a note that cannot be written, nor fretted on the guitar. A quarter tone pitch falls between the half-step placement of the frets and can only be executed on the guitar by bending the string slightly, thus creating a note that lies between the two adjacent frets (A quarter tone bend is noted by a curved arrow with a 1/4 fraction placed above it.) The quarter tone bend can be an important element in blues phrasing for it creates a dirty intonation, and may also be used as a riff.

SLOW BLUES

Slow Blues is a study in phrasing and presents the essence of what blues is all about. Listen to B.B. King and you hear blues played with "feeling". Just watch his facial expression and you know he's *into* his music. B.B. King can get more expression out of one note than any blues guitarist in the business. How is this expression of emotion accomplished? Timing, controlled dynamics, vibrato, bends and slides are the tools. But, the feeling in his music comes from the heart. He "feels" his music. All this too, you may develop if you will take the time to work on the above mentioned aspects of your playing.

ILLUSTRATION ONE

The first measure begins with an eighth note rest. This places the first note on the up-beat (the *and* after the first beat). The first three notes are triplets, played on the second beat. The next note (B) is a quarter note (*one beat*), followed by an eighth note rest, which places the last note (an eighth note) of the measure on the up-beat after the fourth beat. This note is designated as a "hard" note (>). Pick the string a little harder than the other notes. This will give the note more accent as you bend the note into the next measure, which continues the phrase with three eighth notes. This is a fairly straight forward series of notes. A simple riff, but if you can play it in meter and over the shuffle beat and use the expression tools, (the quarter-note and half-note bends and the vibrato) you will hear "the blues".

ILLUSTRATION TWO

In the first measure, the first beat is open, no note and this pause in the phrase adds to the rhythmic feel of the previous measure. The vibrato is a must on the last note, it adds a voice-like quality to the note, an important expression device in blues phrasing. In the second measure, the first note is played on the up-beat after the first beat. It should be struck a little harder than the rest of the notes. Again, this is indicated with the > placed above the note. The ending vibrato *is* a necessity.

ILLUSTRATION THREE – Optional Second Measures

Just to demonstrate how subtle blues phrasing can be, experiment with these optional endings. In the second ending, we have a half-step bend. In the third ending we introduce the bend and release. Pick the first note (B) seventh fret; then, push it up a half-step to the note C; then, on the next beat, lower in a half-step to the note B. The tone should continue ringing through both bends. This double bend, performed properly, creates a special crying sound. You must push with authority to achieve the desired effect. You may have to again experiment with the "comparison" technique in order to train the ear to know when the string has been pushed far enough to achieve the whole-step bend.

A POSITIVE THOUGHT: Rethinking Illustrations 1-2
CUT NOTE (staccato)

These exercises demonstrate how a quarter note bend can be most effective when it is cut short – clipped as it is played. This style of playing a note is called "staccato". A staccato note is not allowed to ring for the indicated duration. This creates a punctuation, and is a definite statement ending device. (The time value of the note is not altered, only the sustain of the tone is changed – it is marked with a dot placed above the effected note). Experiment with this musical device. First pick the note and let it ring until the next note is played, then play it again and clip it short and listen to the difference. We have included the words for these optional measures, try singing them (in your head if need be!), get into the "feel" of lyrical phrasing. It's a great way of learning to make your riffs sing!

SLOW BLUES

A Study in Phrasing

ILLUSTRATION ONE

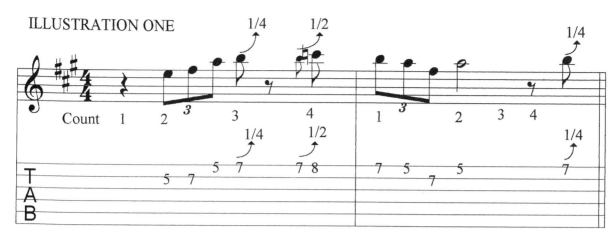

Count   1   2   3   4   1   2   3   4

ILLUSTRATION TWO

First ending

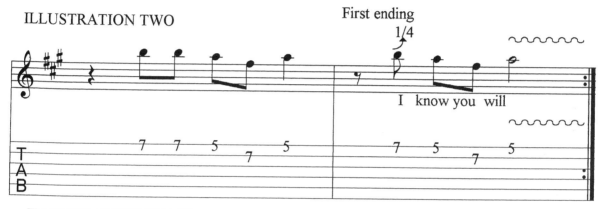

I know you will

ILLUSTRATION THREE

Second ending   Third ending

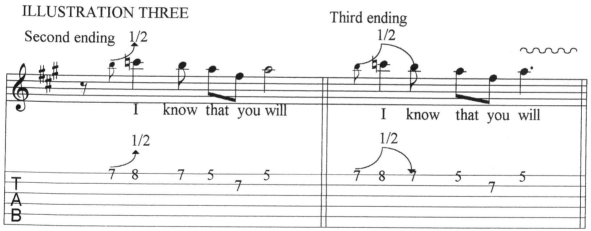

I know that you will   I know that you will

MAKIN' MUSIC

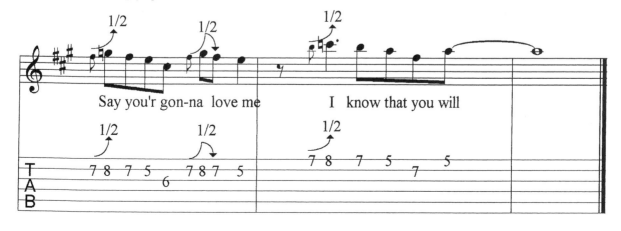

Say you'r gon-na love me   I know that you will

RIFF CONSTRUCTION

The Six Note "Blues Scale"

The scale most often associated with traditional blues music is a variation of the minor pentatonic scale. It is called the "Blues Scale", and is created by adding an additional note, the flat 5th to the five note pentatonic minor scale. This note makes the scale boisterously expressive. It is the "blue" note in blues music. The Blues Scale may be used in a variety of ways. Like its parent pentatonic scale, it can be effective over a dominant chord progression, and may be played over minor harmony (minor chords).

ILLUSTRATION ONE

Illustration One presents the six note Blues Scale played at the fifth fret from the *E* scale form pattern. We have placed a box around the b5. This is the note that creates the blues scale.

ILLUSTRATION TWO

Illustration Two presents a two bar riff using the six note blues scale.

ILLUSTRATION THREE

In Illustration Three, we show the placement of the notes that create the lower octave of the Blues Scale.

MAKIN' MUSIC

Makin' Music is an exercise in playing the lower octave of the Blues Scale.

THE 'SIX NOTE' BLUES SCALE

ILLUSTRATION ONE

ILLUSTRATION TWO

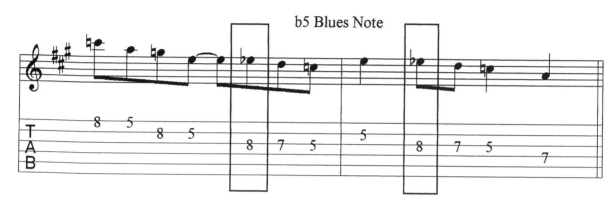

ILLUSTRATION THREE

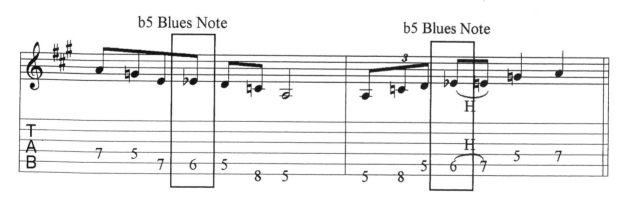

MAKIN' MUISC

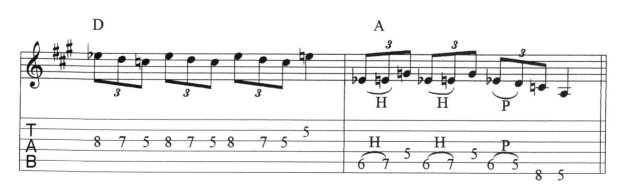

RIFF CONSTRUCTION

Extended Scale Patterns

EXTENDING THE "BOX"

Long stretches of time on a single chord, requires an innovative approach in creating interesting blues solos. While we can create credible sounding solos by changing the rhythmic and harmonic patterns of the pentatonic notes within the standard fixed-position "box", only so much originality can come from the effort. The blues guitarist has several tools at his disposal that he may utilize when creating riffs and solos. He may transpose riffs created within one box pattern to another box pattern. This technique is often used, and in itself, adds variety simply because of the octave shift. He may choose to play from a different chord scale pattern (*CAGED* system). Shifting to a linear movement – playing up and down the strings as opposed to the box pattern adds interest. The simplest approach is to stay in the box position and utilize the scale notes that occur above or below the box.

ILLUSTRATION ONE
UPPER EXTENDATION

In Illustration One, we have written the notes of the *A* minor pentatonic box scale pattern played at the fifth fret. We are using the Blues Scale and have marked the blue note. With a slight hand shift it is possible to play upper extension notes, the note *D* at the tenth fret, first string, and the *E* note at the twelfth fret. **Remember:** By leaving out the blue note, you will be playing a straight *A* minor pentatonic scale. We encourage you to play the scale using both patterns – a great way to develop ear training.

ILLUSTRATION TWO
EXTENDED SCALE PATTERN – LOWER NOTES

In Illustration Two, we have written the notes of the *A* minor pentatonic box scale pattern played at the fifth fret, one octave lower. Again, this is the Blues Scale and we have marked the blue note. We have also marked the blue note in the lower octave for your reference. We recommend using the fingering patterns as indicated by the numbers placed under the TAB-staff.

ILLUSTRATION THREE
LOWER NOTES OPTIONAL FINGERING PATTERN

The third note of the scale, the note *C* natural, played at the eight fret, sixth string is within easy reach. When used, this placement allows a lower octave riff to include the *C* natural note without shifting position, and still end on the *A* note, fifth fret. However, to include the lower octave *G* natural, we must make an awkward hand shift (Illustration Two). In Illustration Three, we show another possibility. We may play the *C* natural on the fifth string, third fret. This does require a hand shift, moving the first finger back to the third fret. However, this facilitates an easier fingering movement when playing the lower note *A* and the lower note *G* natural. When playing the lower scale notes, we are shifting position and this requires shifting the hand. We have indicated the finger shift by marking the shift note with a "slide line". We recommend using the finger pattern as indicated by the numbers placed under the the TAB-staff.

We have placed a box around the note *C* natural to indicate the optional fingering pattern.

EXTENDING THE SCALE

Box pattern 5th fret

ILLUSTRATION ONE   Extended A minor pentatonic blues scale

ILLUSTRATION TWO   ENTENDED SCALE PATTERN - LOWER NOTES

ILLUSTRATION THREE
OPTIONAL FINGERING

Riff Construction
with Extended Tones
– Lower Octave

ILLUSTRATION ONE

Illustration One presents another exercise in playing riffs in the lower octave, moving down to the note *G* at the third fret, sixth string. This exercise includes a "position shift", outlined by the position shift box. Play all notes within the box with your first finger positioned at the third fret.

ILLUSTRATION TWO

Illustration Two is a further bass octave study. Again, play all notes within the position shift box at the third fret.

ILLUSTRATION THREE & FOUR

Pay strict attention to the timing, fingering, and where the position shift occurs.

PLAYING TIP

Listen to great blues keyboard artists. The music of a great keyboard stylist has always been a rich source of ideas for blues players.

EXTENDING THE BOX-BASS OCTAVE

ILLUSTRATION ONE

ILLUSTRATION TWO

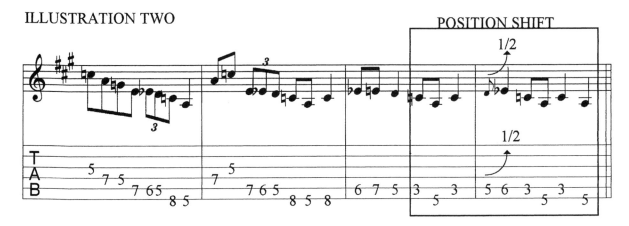

ILLUSTRATION THREE

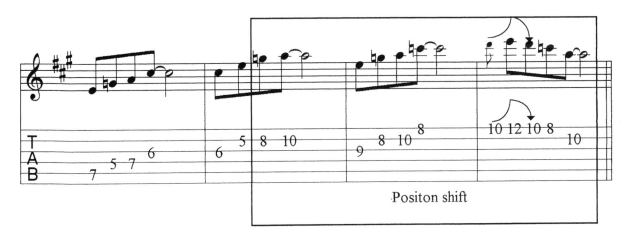

ILLUSTRATION FOUR

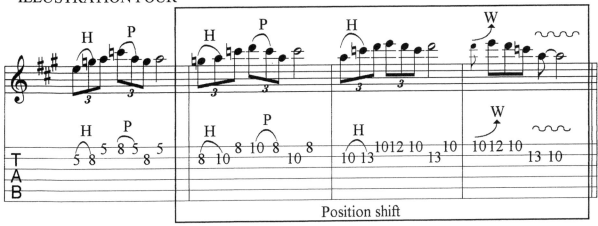

Identifying Chord Tones within the Pentatonic Scale

A7

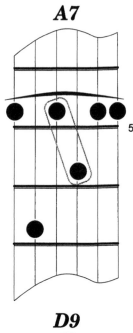

THE IMPORTANCE OF CHORD TONES

As we have previously explained, any pentatonic scale note used to create a riff *will sound correct* when played over the I-IV-V chord progression. However, hot notes used by blues masters to create signature riffs are *"chord tones"*. These tones include: the 1st, 3rd, b7, 9th and 13th notes of the major diatonic scale (page 17). (**Remember:** Not all chord tones appear in the scale.) Chord tones are not always obvious within the pentatonic scale patterns, yet they are revealed by chord shapes! By studying the placement of chord tones within the pentatonic scale, as represented by the shaded circles in Illustration Two, you may more clearly see the physical placement of individual chord notes and how they *lay* within the scale pattern.

D9

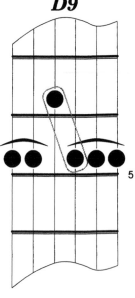

ILLUSTRATION ONE

MINOR PENTATONIC SCALE (Key of *A*)

Illustration One places the five note *A* minor pentatonic scale, *E* chord form pattern, at the fifth fret.

ILLUSTRATION TWO

IDENTIFYING THE CHORD TONES WITHIN THE PENTATONIC SCALE

In Illustration Two, we have circled the chord tones of each chord as they lay within the scale pattern. Below each diagram, we have written the note as they appear on the staff; and below the staff, we have them in TAB.

E9

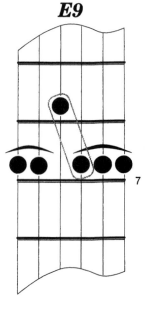

ILLUSTRATION THREE

CHORD SHAPES – TRITONES

The Tritone – In a dominant 7th chord, whether played as 7th, 9th or 13th voicing, the 3rd and b7 degrees form an *interval* that we call a tritone. In blues, the I, IV, V chords are virtually always dominant chords; and when played, in the key of *A*, as *A7, D9* and *E9*, the two note tritone of each chord (illustrations on this page) is made by simply moving the fingering position between the fourth, fifth and sixth frets On the following page, *Illustration Three*, we have written out the tritones for each chord.

IDENTIFYING CHORD TONES WITHIN
THE PENTATONIC SCALE

ILLUSTRATION ONE

PENTATONIC SCALE

ILLUSTRATION TWO

IDENTIFYING CHORD TONES

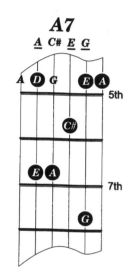

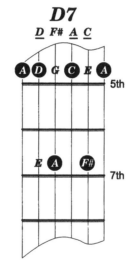

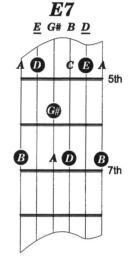

A7   (A) C# (E) (G)

D7 (D) F# (A) (C)

E7   (E) G# B (D)

ILLUSTRATION THREE
TRITONES

A7 3rd C# b7th G

D9 3rd F# b7th C

E7 3rd G# b7 D

RIFF CONSTRUCTION

CHORD TONE RESOLUTION

Of all the "tools" used in creating blues music, none is more important than *the human ear*. There is but one universal rule in blues music that counts: "If it doesn't sound right, it's not right"! Scales, chord tones and the usage of expression tools can only be effectively utilized when you can *hear* the music, the subtle nuances of a partial bend, and a beautiful vibrato. Individual scales determine the placement the notes on the fretboard, and we must place great emphasis on their usage, for it is within this pattern of notes that we can create blues riffs without the fear of playing wrong notes. Implementation of expression tools adds the *flavor* of the blues to scale riffs. However, great riffs are built around the notes that form each chord and it is, therefore, imperative to understand chord tone resolution. In the following exercises, we experiment with riffs incorporating chord tones. Train your ear to hear the subtleties of the tones that create each chord.

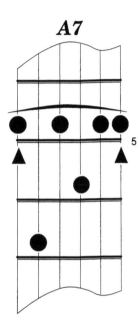

A7

ILLUSTRATION ONE – *A7* (I)

In Illustration One, first measure, we show the notes that form the I chord (key of *A*). In measure two we resolve the note *B*, to the root of the *A7* chord, note *A*. In the third measure we use a hammer-on to resolve to the 3rd, *C#*. In measure five, we resolve to the fifth of the chord, the note *E*. In the last measure we resolve the ♭7 of the *A7* chord, the note *G*.

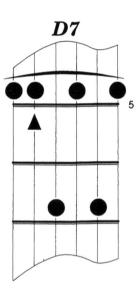

D7

ILLUSTRATION TWO – *D7* (IV)

In Illustration One, first measure, we show the notes that form the IV chord, *D7*. In measure two, we utilize a slide up to the ♭7 of the *D7* chord, then resolve to the root of the chord, note *D*. In the third measure, we resolve to the 3rd, *F#*. In measure five, we resolve to the 5th of the chord, the note *A*. In the last measure, we resolve the ♭7 of the *D7* chord, the note *C*.

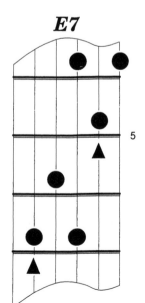

E7

ILLUSTRATION THREE – *E7* (V)

In Illustration One, first measure, we show the notes that form the V chord, *E7* in the key of *A*. In measure two, we utilize a half-step bend, then resolve to the Root tone, the note *E*. In the third measure, we resolve to the 3rd, the *G#*. In the fifth measure, we resolve to the 5th, note *B*. In the last measure, we use a half-step bend, then resolve to the ♭7 of the V chord, the note *D*.

NOTE: Notice how the three chords used in the key of *A*, fall within the "box" scale pattern at the fifth fret.

CHORD TONE RESOLUTION

ILLUSTRATION ONE   Key of A

A7 (I)
A C# E G   Root A   3rd C#   5th E   b7 G

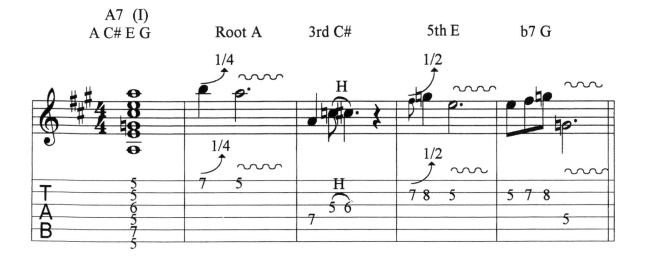

ILLUSTRATION TWO

D7 (IV)
D F# A C   Root D   3rd F#   5th A   b7 C

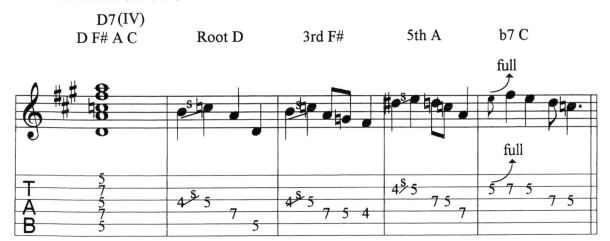

ILLUSTRATION THREE

E7 (V)
E G# B D   Root E   3rd G#   5th B   b7 D

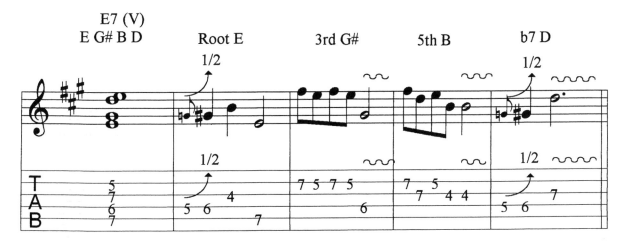

RIFF CONSTRUCTION

I-IV-V Chord Tones

CREATING RIFFS WITH CHORD TONES

The *"secret"* of great blues riffs, lies in the magic of *"chord-tone harmony"*. Implementing *"chord tones"* is a great way to move beyond the minor pentatonic scale notes. Chord tones are essential elements in blues phrasing as they are used to reinforce chord changes and add structure to blues riffs. A basic chord is built upon three tones called a *"triad"*. There are major, minor, dominant, augmentative, and diminished chords (page 00). Chords may be altered or extended. The notes that compromise each type of chord create a specific sound and must be taken into consideration when building riffs. We will limit our study to the dominant seventh chord (1st, 3rd, 5th, and b7) and its extension, the dominant 9th chord.

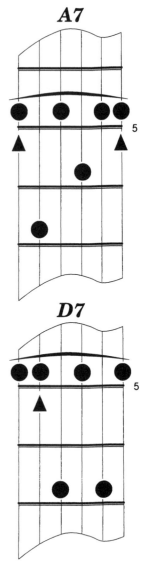

Knowledge of chord triads and the *"extended"* notes that form the dominant seventh, and dominant ninth chords, is imperative in order to build strong riffs. In blues, each of the three chords that appear in the I-IV-V progression are played as a dominant chord and have two or more tones in common with the five note pentatonic scale. We will analyze those dominant chord tones that lie within the pentatonic scale pattern and demonstrate how they are used to create great riffs. In the course of our studies studdies , we will explore how these notes outline chord changes. Remember: Chord tones *"may"* or *"may not"* be a pentatonic scale note.

ILLUSTRATION ONE

In Illustration One, we present the *A* minor pentatonic scale with common notes from the *A7* chord outlined in boxes. Practice playing the scale, and use one of the *A7* chord tones as the last note. Play the chord and listen to the harmonic relationship of the scale against the chord.

ILLUSTRATION TWO

In Illustration Two, we have outlined the chord tones of the D7 chord. We include the 9th tone, the note *E*, which provides an additional chord tone we may utilize in creating a riff over the D7 chord. Practice creating riffs that resolve on one of the chord tones.

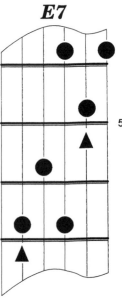

ILLUSTRATION THREE

In Illustration Three, we outline the two notes of the *E7* chord that appear within the *A* minor pentatonic scale. Again, create riffs that resolve to one of the chord tones and listen to the strong harmonic pull to the tonal center of the chord.

I-IV-V CHORD TONES

ILLUSTRATION ONE

A7 CHORD TONES

1 3 5 b7
A C# E G

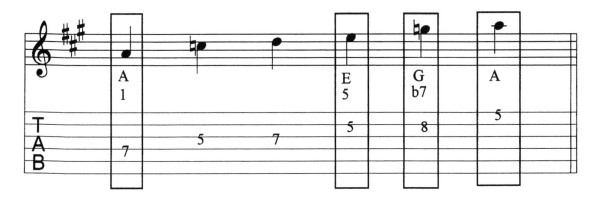

ILLUSTRATION TWO

D7 CHORD TONES

1 3 5 b7 9
D F# A C E

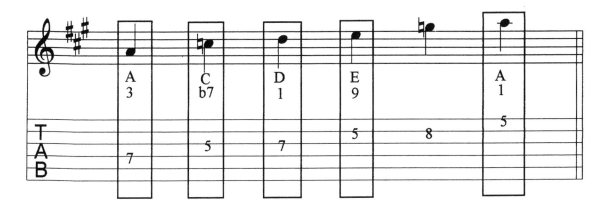

ILLUSTRATION THREE

E7 CHORD TONES

1 3 5 b7
E G# B D

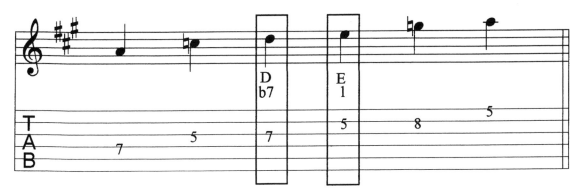

Riff Construction

CHORD TONE RESOLUTION

The application and possibilities of creating riffs with chord tones are limitless. In order to apply all of the concepts that may be used in riff construction, we must concern ourselves with the proper application of chord tones. In the following exercises we have created a sequence of riffs that end on a chord tone.

When practicing these riffs, listen to the internal tension/release patterns. It is important to remember that individual riffs must be connected to other riffs played across chord changes.

Since each chord tone can effect the harmonic structure of the riff as it relates to the chord over which it is being played, you must learn how to incorporate the proper chord tone in order to make your musical ideas take your ear where you want it to go.

Play it at a medium tempo and familiarize youself with the character of each pitch and concentrate on the harmonic color of each tone and how it effects your ear, for as you will discover, some chord tones create resolution while others stay the same. Play each riff and consider the relationship of the chord tone and the rhythm chord over which the riff is played, and how each chord tone changes the harmonic context of the riff itself.

ILLUSTRATION ONE & TWO

In Illustrations One and Two, we have created a riff for the I chord, *A7*. Each riff ends on a chord triad tone: the b7, 3rd, and 5th of the chord.

ILLUSTRATIONS THREE & FOUR

In Illustrations Three and Four, we created riffs for the IV chord, D9. Each riff ends with a chord triad tone: the b7, 1st, 3rd, and 5th of the chord. We incorporate the minor third, *F* natural (scale note) and the major third, *F* sharp of the chord (chord tone). This minor/major third is utilized as passing tone. Passing tones are great ways to bridge scale notes and chord tones.

CHORD TONE RESOLUTION

ILLUSTRATION ONE

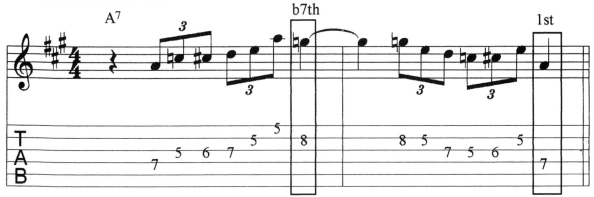

ILLUSTRATION TWO

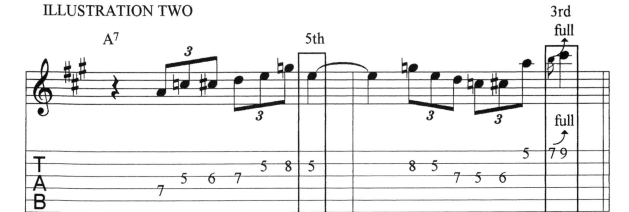

ILLUSTRATION THREE

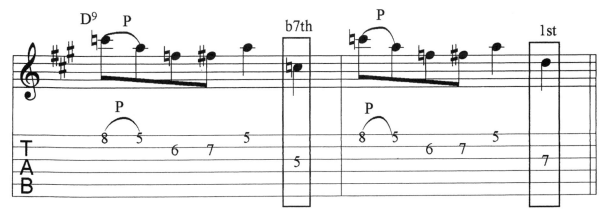

ILLUSTRATION FOUR

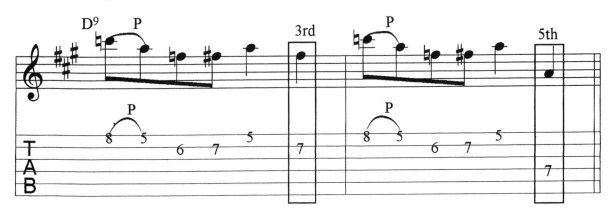

Three Ways to Make the "Scale-chord" Transition

While it is possible to play riffs utilizing the notes of the proper minor pentatonic scale without regard to the chords in the blues progression, as we have previously explained, it is preferable to create riffs that employ chord tones. It is necessary to know how to create a riff that moves smoothly from the tonal characteristics of one chord into the harmonic color of the following chord. There are three ways to create a smooth chord transition (playing the chord change): **1.** lead into a riff with a common tone, **2.** lead into a riff with the tonic note of the next chord, or **3.** lead into a riff by implementing "passing tones".

ILLUSTRATION ONE
COMMON TONES

In our studies of chord tones, we have demonstrated how individual chord tones lie within the minor pentatonic scale. There is a minimum of two common tones in any two connected chords within the blues chord progression. And, we may end a riff on one of these common tones, and then begin the next riff with this tone. This will telegraph the new chord.

ILLUSTRATION TWO
TONIC NOTE OF THE FOLLOWING CHORD

We may end a riff with a note that may be a non-scale tone, but is a note of the next chord. This is often called the "leading tone" concept. The strongest chord tone is the root note (1), a great note to begin a riff over a chord change.

PASSING TONES

Another great transitional tool is the implementation of "passing tones". Passing tones are notes of brief duration that lead to a chord tone. A great device to accomplish this transition is to use a half-step movement. This half-step movement is at the heart of the "minor melody-against-major harmony" theoretical concept. (Minor third of the pentatonic scale and the major third of the dominant chord.)

SCALE-CHORD TRANSITION

ILLUSTRATION ONE
COMMON TONE

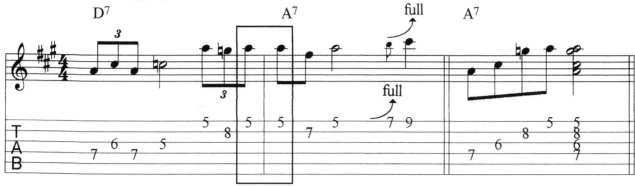

ILLUSTRATION TWO

TONIC NOTE OF FOLLOWING CHORD

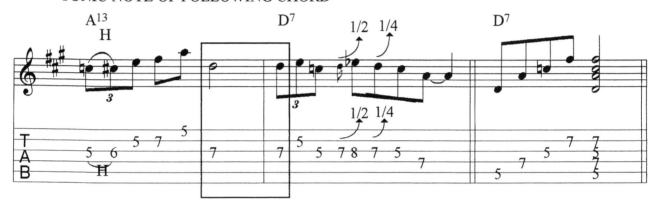

NOTE OF FOLLOWING CHORD

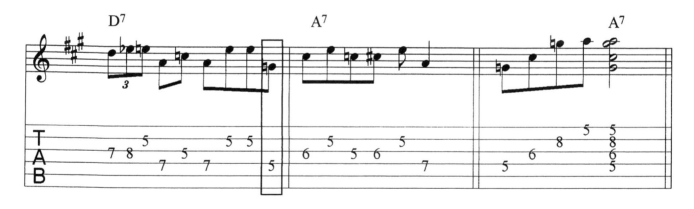

PASSING TONES

Blues Solo One
Exercise in Tone Resolution

Now, we bring together all the elements of riff construction: a 12-bar chord progression, the minor pentatonic scale, and expression tools (the bends, hammer-ons and slides). We incorporate just enough notes to make the phrases interesting and we encourage you to analyze how each measure resolves to individual chord tones. It is also important to "feel" the rhythm of the shuffle beat, for without this all important aspect of playing blues, all the notes in the world will not make a solo come alive.

A POSITIVE THOUGHT: Blues Solo One

Blues Solo One is written to be played over a slow "shuffle" rhythm pattern. We encourage you to practice playing over one of the appropriate *Blues Jam Tracks* included on the accompanying CD. Or, you may want to have a friend play a shuffle rhythm pattern for you. A great way of learning is to play with live accompaniment. You *must* learn to phrase over the shuffle beat.

SOLO ONE
Chord Tone Resolution

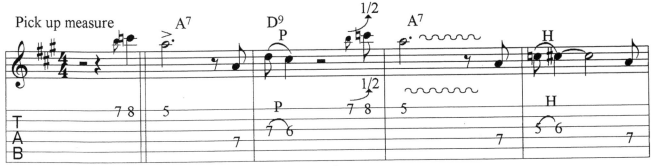

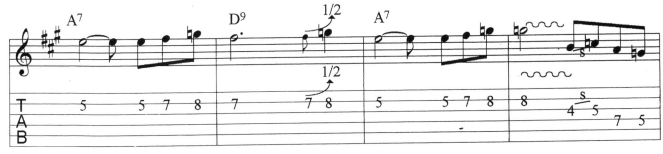

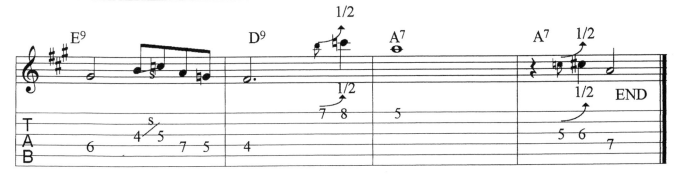

Mastering the I-IV Chord Change

At the heart of the "blues chord progression" is the I-IV chord change. This change happens three times in the standard "quick change" 12-bar progression. It occus between measures 1-2, 4-5, and 10-11. Previously, we have demonstrated how one riff may be played over both chords, however this approach often sounds superficial and lacks harmonic color. A better approach is to outline each chord melodically by targeting individual chord tones. By accenting the "major-minor" relationship of the minor scale over the major chord, we find that it is possible to play one riff across both chords. In the key of *A,* these two notes are: *C-C#.* These two notes virtually define their respective scale and chord. By targeting the major third of the I chord and the dominant seventh of the IV chord, the sound of the I-IV chord change is reinforced. Also, playing either one of these notes on the first beat of a measure creates a strong chordal identification and, when utilized effectively, enables one to more readily hear the chord changes.

ILLUSTRATION ONE

The second note of the *A* minor pentatonic scale is *C* natural.

ILLUSTRATION TWO

This "scale tone" (*C* natural) is the dominant seventh (flat seventh) of the IV chord *D7-D F# A (C).* The third of the *A7* chord is *C#-A (C#) E G,* and lies a half-step above the *A* minor pentatonic scale's second note (*C* natural). This half-step movement is at the heart of the minor scale against major scale concept.

ILLUSTRATION THREE

The dominant seventh (flat seventh) of the IV chord *D7,* is the note *C* natural. This "chord tone" is the second note of the *A* minor pentatonic scale.

NOTE: Arpeggios outline the chord tones in examples two and three.

I-IV CHORD CHANGE

ILLUSTRATION ONE
  SCALE TONES
  A minor pentatonic scale

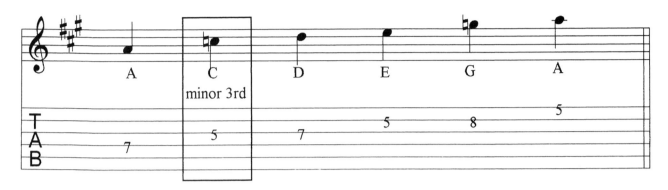

ILLUSTRATION TWO
  CHORD TONES
  (1) CHORD A9   A C# E G B

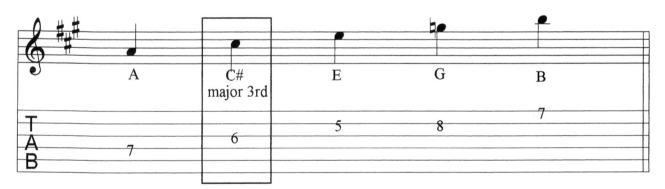

ILLUATRATION THREE
  CHORD TONES
  (IV) CHORD D9   D F# A C E

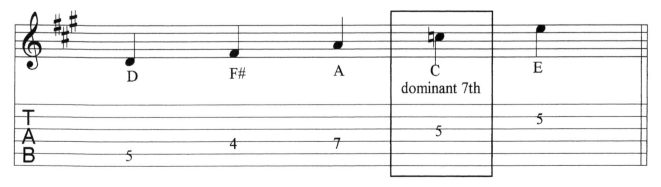

Mastering the I-IV Chord Change
Major Third-Dominant Seventh

It is important to realize how these two notes function in riff construction for either note "will" sound correct when incorporated into a solo created from the notes of the *A* minor pentatonic scale. By targeting the correct note, we can establish the tonality of the chord and lead the ear on to the next chord change. In the following exercises, we experiment with this *C* to *C#* - minor/major tonality. We feature the *C#* in riffs developed for the *A7th* chord, and we use *C* in riffs developed for the *D7th* chord.

ILLUSTRATION ONE

In the first measure we feature the note *C#*, and it is meant to be played over the I chord *(A7)*. The second measure features the note *C*, and is meant to be played over the IV chord *(D9)*. We end the first measure with the note *A*, the root of the *A7*.

ILLUSTRATION TWO

We begin measure with a slide up to *C#* (chord tone) the fifth of *A7*, and end on *G*, the dominant seventh tone. In the second measure we again utilize a slide, up to *C*, the 9th of *D9* chord, and the resolve to the note *A*, the fifth of the *D9*.

ILLUSTRATION THREE

We begin measure one with *C#*, the fifth of the *A7* chord (third string-seventh fret), and resolve to the *A* on the first string. In measure two, we use hammer-on *C* (scale tone) to note *D* (chord tone) the root of the *D7* chord. We resolve the second measure with a hammer-on C (chord tone) and the dominant seventh of *D7*, to *C#* (chord tone) the fifth of *A7*.

ILLUSTRATION FOUR

We begin measure one on the *C#* and finish the measure on the *A*, first string. We begin the second measure with a hammer-on, *F* to *F#*, the fifth, and end the measure on the note *D*, the root tone of *D9*.

MAJOR THIRD-DOMINANT SEVENTH
Chord Tone Resolution

ILLUSTRATION ONE

ILLUSTRATION TWO

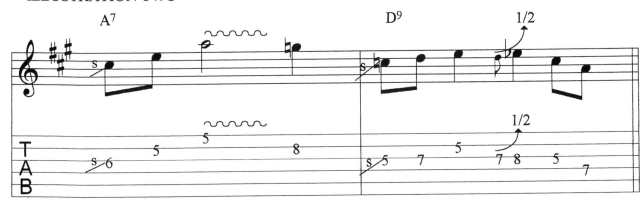

ILLUSTRATION THREE

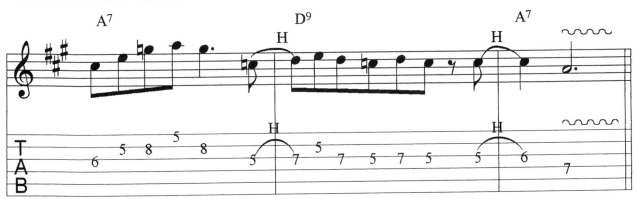

ILLUSTRATION FOUR

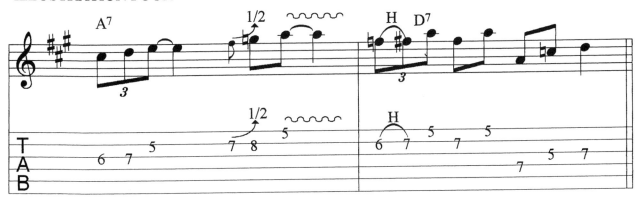

RIFF CONSTRUCTION

Mastering the I-IV Chord Change

ILLUSTRATION ONE

Measure one begins with a hammer-on, *C* to *C#* (scale tone to chord tone), and resolves on the root note of the I chord, the noted *A*. Measure two begins with a scale tone, the note *B*, and then moves to a chord tone *C*, the dominant seventh tone of the IV chord, *D9*.

ILLUSTRATION TWO

Measure one features the movement between the major third-minor third *C* to *C#* (scale tone-chord tone). In measure two, the tonal center is based upon the note *C*, the dominant seventh tone in the *D9* chord. It resolves to a note common to both chords, the note *A* (fifth of *D9*, the root of *A7*).

ILLUSTRATION THREE

Measure one begins with a bend, *C* to *C#* (major-minor movement). The tonal center of this measure is the note *C#*, the third of the *A7* chord. The second measure begins with a large interval pull-off, *C* to the note *A*, the fifth of the IV chord *D9*, and resolves to the root of the *D9* chord, the note *D*.

ILLUSTRATION FOUR

In this exercise, we demonstrate how simple it is to play a riff that features the *C* to *C#* major/minor tonal movement that defines the *A7* and *D9* chord. In the second measure, the note *C* (dominant tone), defines the IV chord, *D9*. The measure ends on the note *E*, the 9th of the IV chord.

ILLUSTRATION FIVE

In this exercise, we repeat the basic note pattern used in Illustration four. We incorporate a pull-off to bridge the resolution between the I chord and *A7*, and the IV chord *D9*.

NOTE: In all of these examples, notice how the first finger is used as a "bridge" to "roll" from string to string. This is a blues technique that must be performed very smoothly to be effective. Listen to the examples and try to emulate the smoothness.

MASTERING THE I-IV CHORD CHANGE

ILLUSTRATION ONE

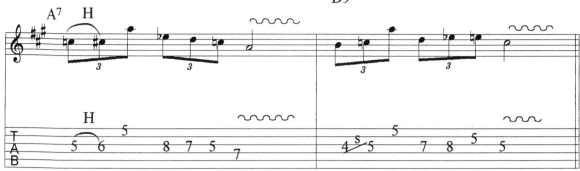

ILLUSTRATION TWO

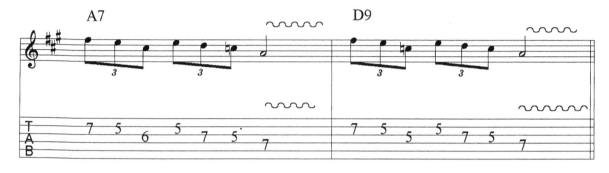

ILLUSTRATION THREE

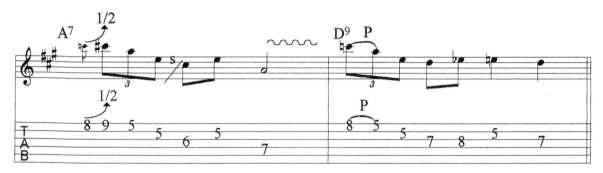

ILLUSTRATION FOUR

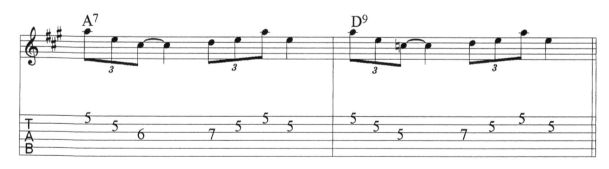

ILLUSTRATION FIVE

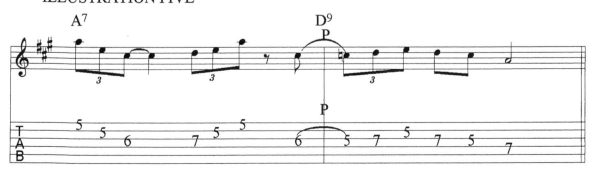

Tritone Development

In blues, the I-IV-V chords are virtually always dominant chords. (7ths, 9ths, 13ths) The tritone interval consisting of the third and flat seventh (3rd-b7) defines the dominant sound, which has become a staple in blues music.

ILLUSTRATION ONE

The first three notes, played as triplets, lead in to the tritones interval that defines the A7 (I) chord. The same triplet is used to lead the ear into the D7 (IV) chord's tritone. We have used slides as a device to play the tritones.

ILLUSTRATION TWO

Illustration Two is an example of how double steps may be used in innovative riff construction. In this example, we use double stops played as triplets, and as passing tones leading to the A7 tritone in the second measure. Again, we use double stops played as triplets to lead us to the D7 tritone in the third measure.

ILLUSTRATION THREE

Illustration Three utilizes triplets to move from the I chord to the IV chord tritone in the second measure. Again, in measure two, we utilize triplets to move to the IV chord tritone.

MAKIN' MUSIC

Listen to the tonal movement between chord changes. Train your ears to identify the individual chord tritones.

A POSITIVE THOUGHT

Should you play E7 or E9? Either chord is correct! The choice of chord is really a choice of fingering preference, and or harmonic color.

TRITONE DEVELOPMENT

ILLUSTRATION ONE

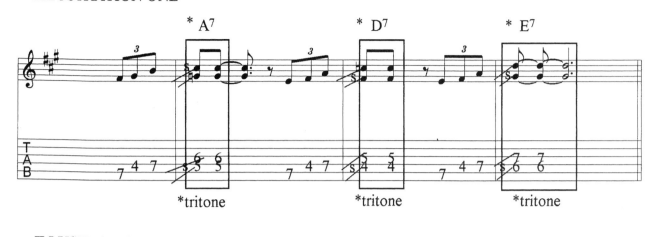

ILLUSTRATION TWO

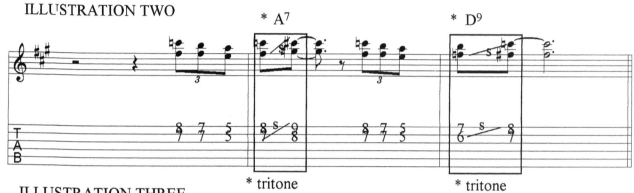

ILLUSTRATION THREE

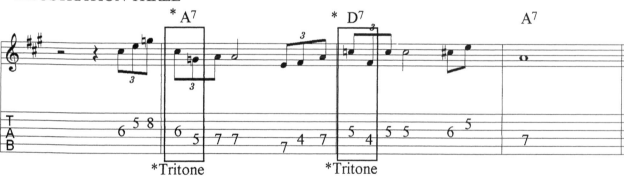

MAKIN' MUSIC

Mastering the I-V Chord Change

The I to V chord change occurs between the 8th and 9th measure in the 12 bar blues progression. The V chord, played either as a 7th or 9th (in the key of *A: E7-E9*), is an unstable chord and is used to move music between the I chord and the IV chord. In the standard blues chord progression, it is a "one" measure chord change. In order to fully understand the application of the V chord in blues, we must first identify the chord tones of the V chord and its placement within the pentatonic scale. We covered this subject in "Chord Tone Resolution". Now, we will further expand on the tonal application of the V chord in riff construction.

ILLUSTRATION ONE

There are only two V chord (*E7*) tones within the *A* minor pentatonic scale. They are the notes *E* (root) and *D* (flat seventh). That's not a lot of notes with which to create music! The addition of the *E* chord's major third chord tone *G#*, offers additional possibilities. In chord construction, the major third establishes the chord's *major* tonal characteristics (as opposed to the minor characteristic). The addition of the major third chord tone establishes a strong melodic element that expands our ability to create an effective riff over the V chord. While it is permissible to play a *G* pentatonic scale note (scale tone) over *E* type chords (*E7-E9*), it should be a passing tone. However, there are times when the *G* natural sounds great when a lot of tension is desired. *G* natural added to the *E9* chord forms and *E7* (#9) chord and creates tension in the harmony.

ILLUSTRATION TWO

It is more desirable to outline the chord melodically when creating riffs by targeting the V chord's major third (chord tone), *G#*. The fifth note of the *A* minor pentatonic scale is *G* natural, a minor tonality. We may move from the scale tone, *G* natural, to the chord tone *G#*, by the application of half-step expression tools. Example: Half-step bend, half-step slide, half-step hammer-ons. This minor-major (scale tone/chord tone) half-step relationship is a great expression note.

I-V CHORD CHANGE

ILLUSTRATION ONE

A minor pentonic scale

E7 chord tones - E G# B D

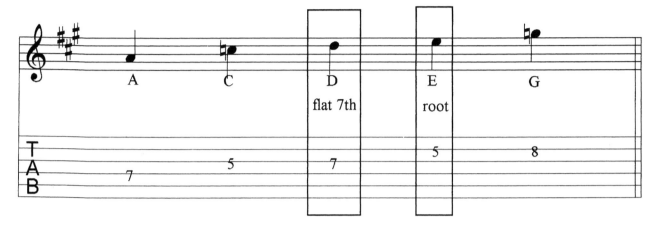

ILLUSTRATION TWO

E9 chord tones - E G# B D F#

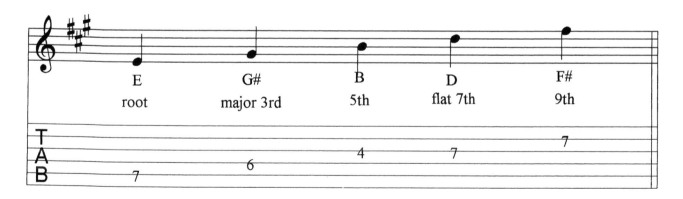

RIFF CONSTRUCTION

Mastering the V-IV Chord Change

The ninth bar of the twelve bar blues progression is a V chord, and resolves to the IV chord at the tenth bar. As we have demonstrated previously, the V chord incorporates only two notes of the pentatonic scale, the root of chord E, which is the fifth note of the A minor pentatonic scale, and the note D, the dominant seventh tone of the chord. In the ninth measure of the V chord is a "stand alone" chord, and from this measure the progression gravitates, passing through the IV, back to the I chord in the eleventh measure. The ninth measure is actually the ending of an eight bar phrase. In riff construction, the first two beats of the ninth measure is used to finalize the eight bar phrase. The third and fourth beats are used to setting up the riff to be played in the tenth measure. The IV chord leads the ear to the last two measures of the twelve bar progression, which is used as the "turnaround", or ending statement. With the limited number of beats to play over, it is important to understand how to play with a few notes that are effective in moving the progression on to the next measure.

ILLUSTRATION ONE

In exercise 1a, we use the V chord to move the riff in to the next measure which is the IV chord. There are many ways this may be accomplished, including the usage of chromatic tones. In exercise 1b, we start with a hammer-on, play a third interval, and move on to the root of the D9 chord.

ILLUSTRATION TWO

In exercise 2a, we use a triplet at the end of the first measure and pull-off in the second measure moving to the root of the D9 chord. In exercise 2b, we use two sets of triplets in the first measure and move to a whole step bend in the second measure, ending on the third of D9 chord which is played as a hard tone.

ILLUSTRATION THREE

In exercise 3a, we utilize tri-tones to emphasize the chord tones of the E9 and D9 chords. In exercise 3b, we incorporate chord tones played as arpeggios.

ILLUSTRATION FOUR

In exercise 4a, we incorporate major arpeggios. In 4b, we simply vary the theme in a higher octave.

V-IV CHORD CHANGE

ILLUSTRATION ONE

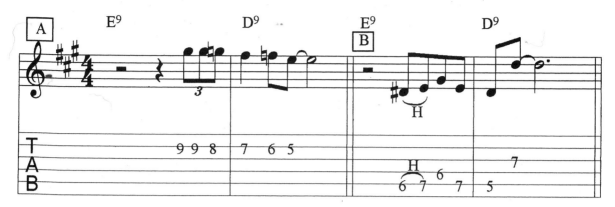

ILLUSTRATION TWO

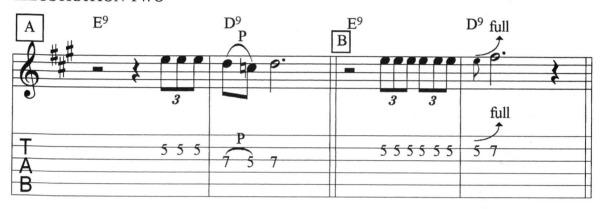

ILLUSTRATION THREE

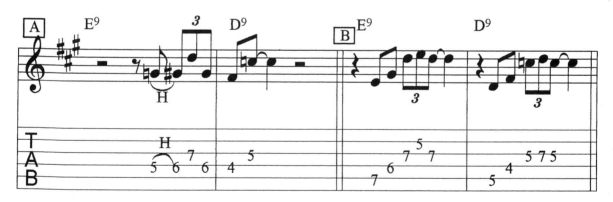

ILLUSTRATION FOUR

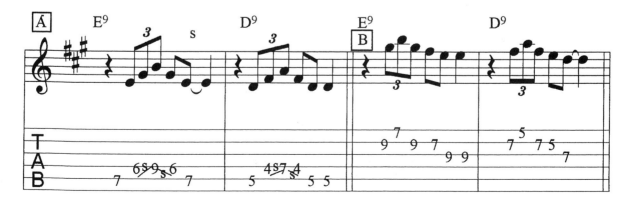

SOMETHING TO THINK ABOUT

SHIFTING KEYS WHEN YOU DON'T KNOW WHAT YOUR DOING

Play your favorite lick, riff, or phrase. In what key are you playing? What if you were asked to play the same pattern in a different key, could you? Are you playing open string notes—E A D G B E? If not, then you can readily change keys. How? All scales and chords move chromatically on the guitar fretboard. When playing a closed chord, scale pattern, or riff, (no open strings), the same fingering pattern can be played at any fret and this shifts keys. Most anyone that has played guitar for a while is familiar with 'bar chords', called closed chords. Any scale pattern or groups of notes that does not contain open string tones moves chromatically just like closed chords. A lick played in the key of *A*, can just as readily be played in the key of *B♭, C, G,* or any other scale pattern that does not contain open strings.

"Okay, I'm playing in the key of A, tenth fret, pentatonic box," you say, "but at what fret would I find the key of C?" Simple! Follow the second string chromatic scale. A riff played at the tenth fret, key of A, would be in the key of C when played at the thirteenth fret. Question to ask—in the chromatic scale, how many half-steps (guitar frets) between A and C? Answer—three half steps.

Remember: everything moves *chromatically.*

Something to think about.

Riff in the key of A

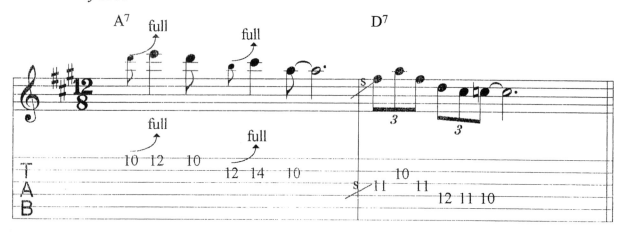

Same riff in the key of C

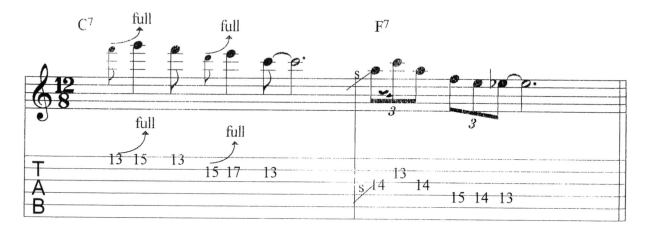

162

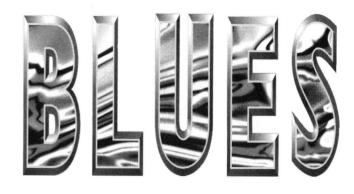

BEGINNINGS

TURNAROUNDS

ENDINGS

MUSIC

The Greeks were the first known people in history to think about music systematically. There were few areas of music creation of which they were not aware. They were familiar with the technique of composing, they understood the need for a system of musical notation. The word music is derived from the Greek word "mousa", meaning "muse". The Muses were the nine goddesses, daughters of Zeus.

The Greeks experimented with many forms of music, however, most of their music was based on the "tetrachord", a system of four note scales called "modes". They developed the first understanding of pitch, the frequency of notes. The word "octave", is from the Greek, "oktko", the number eight. The diatonic octave is two, four note tetrachords. The word "note" comes from the Greek word "neuma", which means "figure", or "sign".

The Greek philosopher and mathematician, Pythagoras, is believed to have discovered the fundamental laws of sound. Using a single string instrument called a Kanon, he discovered how to create intervals of the musical scale, the basic interval of the octave. The Kanon was a long sound-box over which a string was stretched. The string was supported by a movable bridge by which the length of the vibrating string could be increased or shortened allowing the exact measurements of intervals.

During the thirteenth century, two instruments evolved from the lute family — the Guitarra Morica, *and* Guitarra Latina. *The guitarra morica had a pronounced arched back and in the fifteenth century became the* Mandola, *an instrument with four double strings, the forerunner of our modern mandolin.*

The guitarra latina, with its flat back and oval belly curving to a point at the top led to the development, in the thirteenth century, of the Viheula, *an instrument with a flat sound-box, short backward bent neck, and a peg box mounted at an angle.*

During the Classical period, the curvature of the sound-box became more pronounced and the guitar was strung with double courses (pairs of strings), a Spanish influence. At this time, the French and Italians used single courses which were easier to tune, and in time, they came to be the standard string set for later guitars.

The early sixteenth century guitar had four gut strings. In the second half of the century, the fifth and sixth strings appeared, expanding the instrument tonal range.

Because of the Spanish influence in guitar design, the pinched waist, sound-hole design and placement, and written compositions for the Guitarra Esponolo — *the guitar became known as the* Spanish Guitar.

Beginnings–Turnarounds–Endings

A blues arrangement must have a **beginning** (called an *intro*), the body of the song – the *verses*, a **turnaround** (to repeat choruses), and an **ending** (with which to end the song). A beginning may be as simple as a count-off, or it may be a one- or two-bar phrase that ends on the I chord. Each verse of a blues song is only 12 measures long; and is, therefore, repeated a number of times. These repeat verses are facilitated by a device called a *turnaround*, which will always end on the V chord (this demands resolution to the I chord). Of course, every song must come to an end. The ending is most often a statement, or proclamation, that brings the song to a solid finality. This is accomplished by ending on the I chord. A beginning, turnaround or ending may be a simple riff designed to fulfill these tasks. And as you will come to realize, a carefully crafted riff may serve all three purposes!

BEGINNINGS – PICK-UP NOTES

There are four standard ways of beginning a blues song: (1) by playing the entire 12-bar blues change until the vocalist begins singing; (2) by playing the turnaround of the song as the beginning riff; (3) by playing the song from the V chord (called *from the five*) through the turnaround back to the beginning; or (4) by playing a *vamp*. A vamp is when the band plays rhythm on the I chord or a group of chords, until the vocal begins.

A song may also kick off with a short burst of notes, which are usually triplets, played on the preceding beat leading to the first beat of the first measure. These notes are called *pick-up* notes, or *kick-off riff*, and are borrowed from the last measure of the arrangement. A pick-up phrase may be played with single notes, double notes or even three notes. Chord fragments (called partial chords) may also be utilized.

TURNAROUNDS

The **turnaround** is defined as a musical device that facilitates the movement of an arrangement from the end back to the beginning. A turnaround may be one or two measures in length and will most often utilize dominant seventh chords. The usage of dominant seventh chords creates tension that resolves back to the tonic chord in the first measure of the first line of music. The turnaround also has the effect of preparing the player for the next verse. It also lets the listener know that the next lyrical phrase is about to begin.

Theoretically, the turnaround is a one- or two-bar phrase, incorporating the eleventh and twelfth measures in a blues progression; and may be constructed with single notes, double notes, complete chords or chord fragments. Complex turnarounds employ elements of each, plus a classical musical device called *contrary motion* (a series of tones moving in ascending or descending order against a fixed tone). As with many blues phrases, turnarounds may be embellished with *bends, vibrato, pull-offs* and *hammer-ons*. A turnaround may be picked with down strokes, up strokes, or by utilizing the alternating picking technique. Listen to your favorite blues song and learn to identify the beginnings and turnarounds.

BEGINNINGS-TURNAROUNDS-ENDINGS

Tags

A tag is defined as a short musical statement usually of one or two beats that normally occurs at the end of the twelfth measure. It may either be a series of notes or a cluster of chords. Tags are always embedded in the turnaround phrase. The tonality of the tag either ends the song or establishes a tonal movement that returns the song to the first measure. In this manner, a turnaround may be used to begin a song, repeat verses, or end the piece. If a tag ends on the he V7 chord, the eleventh and twelfth measures are considered a turnaround to the first measure of the arrangement. If the tag ends on the I chord, the eleventh and twelfth measures are considered the ending.

ILLUSTRATION ONE
BEGINNING TAG ("KICK-OFF" RIFF)

In Illustration One, we present a turnaround as a simple beginning phrase. It is tagged with notes of the V chord. A triplet pick-up phrase moves the music to the I chord in the first measure of the song.

ILLUSTRATION TWO
TURNAROUND TAG

In Illustration Two, the same phrase is used as a turnaround in the eleventh and twelfth measures. This *ending tag*, is comprised of the notes of the V chord *E7*. Pick-up notes move the music back to the first measure of the song.

ILLUSTRATION THREE
ENDING TAG

In Illustration Three, we again use the same turnaround phrase. However, we now use a tag that resolves to the root note of the I chord, therefore ending the piece.

REMEMBER: You must develop the *feel* of the shuffle rhythm. Play these examples slowly and practice again proper shuffle beats on the accompanying Audio CD.

TAGS

ILLUSTRATION ONE
BEGINNING TAG "Kick-off" riff

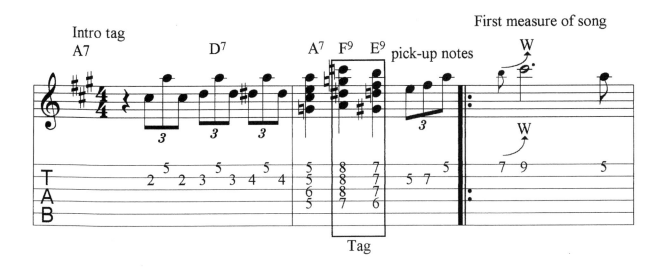

ILLUSTRTION TWO

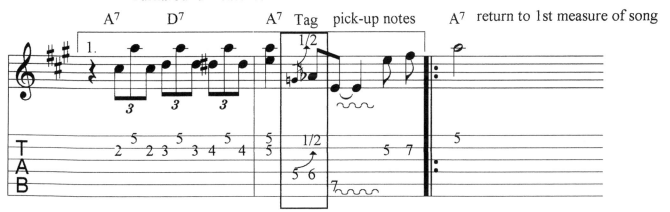

ILLUSTRATION THREE

Ending riff

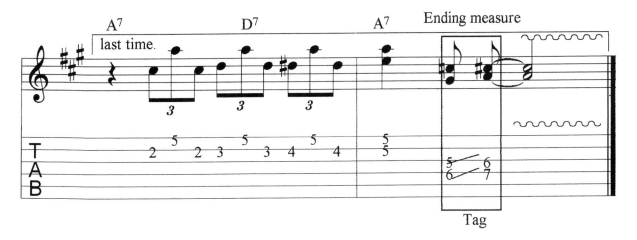

Ending Tags

In the following examples we demonstrate turnarounds, each with an ending tag, that are either a pattern of notes, or a group of chords the harmonize the I chord. The I chord is the strongest chord in an arrangement for it is the first, or tonic chord of the key in which the song is played, and it normally begins and ends a song.

ILLUSTRATION ONE

In Illustration One, the chord progression moves from the I7, IV9 to the I7. The example ends on the tonic note of the key, or root note of the I chord, the note *A*. Ending a passage on the tonic, or first note of the key, establishes the finality required to end a song.

ILLUSTRATION TWO

In Illustration Two, we use triples played in descending order, moving from the I7 chord through the IV9 chord (eleventh measure) and resolving to the I7 chord (twelfth measure). We then use a half-step descending choral movement *Bb13*, to end on *A13*.

ILLUSTRATION THREE

In Illustration Three, we move from the I7 chord, eleventh measure to an ascending half-step choral movement in measure twelve – *G7-G#7* to *A7*.

ILLUSTRATION FOUR

In Illustration Four, we use a descending single note movement leading to the ending tag. The new tag is accomplished by playing a chord a half-step above the tonic, *Bb9* to *A9*. This is a "double" tag! In the twelfth measure, we first tag *A7, E9, A7*. Then we tag again by starting one half step above the I chord by playing *Bb9*, and then resolve to *A9*.

ENDING TAGS

ILLUSTRATION ONE

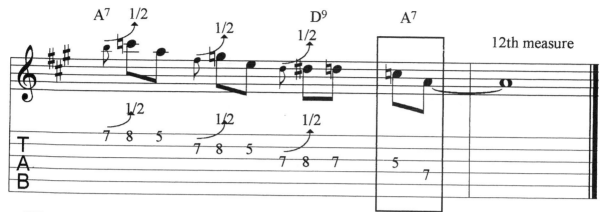

ILLUSTRATION TWO

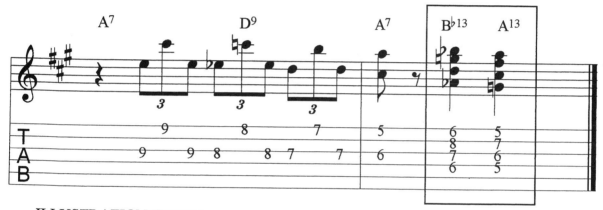

ILLUSTRATION THREE

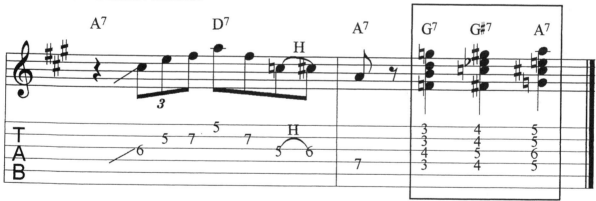

ILLUSTRATION FOUR

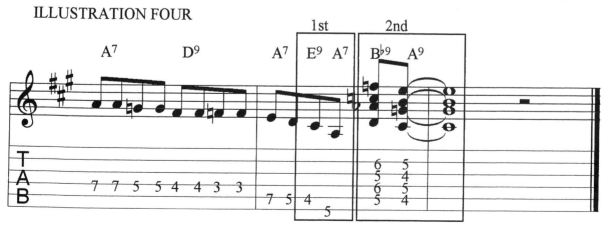

BEGINNINGS-TURNAROUNDS-ENDINGS

Turnaround Examples
in Various Keys

Turnarounds are an important part of blues music and we strongly recommend that you learn as many variations as possible. The more tunrarounds in your *bag of tricks*, the less likely your playing will become boring! A good turnaround can drive the music forward and serve as a jumping-off point for new and original solos. On the following pages, we present a series of turnarounds in the keys of *A, E, D, C* and *G*. In these examples, we end the turnaround with a V chord tag. We have also utilized the implementation of chords – the #V to V, (sharp V to natural V), a favorite tag used by blues musicians to establish the turnaround phrase.

> **REMEMBER:** All examples must
> be played over a shuffle beat.

---PLAYING TIP---
Eliminate what doesn't work and concentrate on the notes that best express your feelings.

TURNAROUNDS

Turnarounds in the Key of A

TURNAROUNDS IN _A_

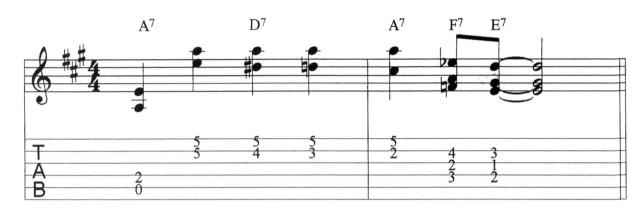

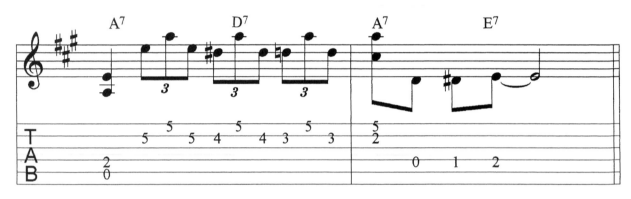

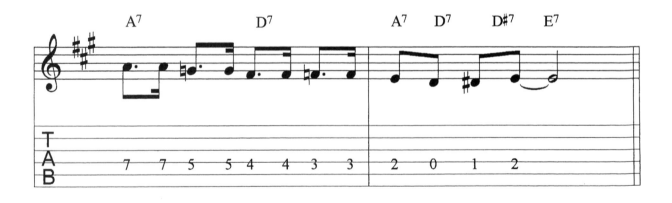

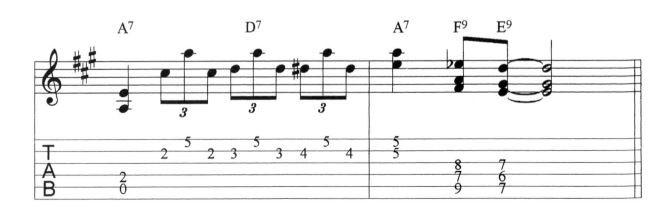

TURNAROUNDS

TURNAROUNDS IN 'E'

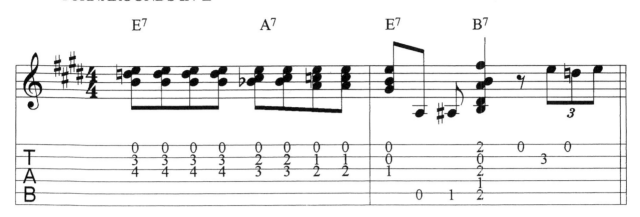

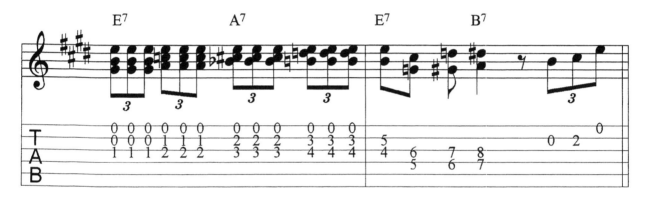

TURNAROUNDS IN 'D'

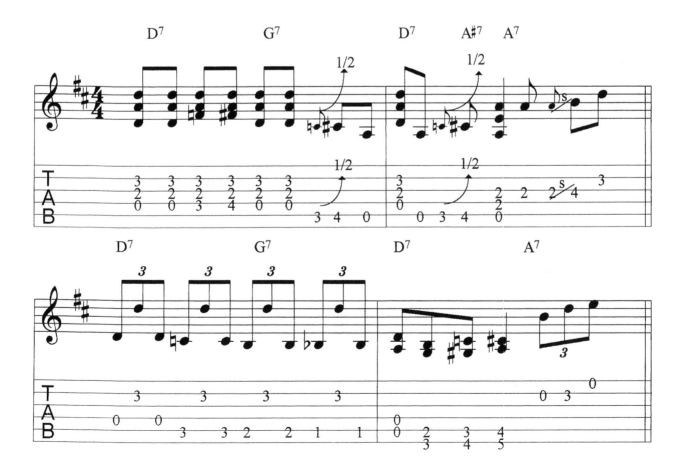

TURNAROUNDS

TURNAROUNDS IN 'C'

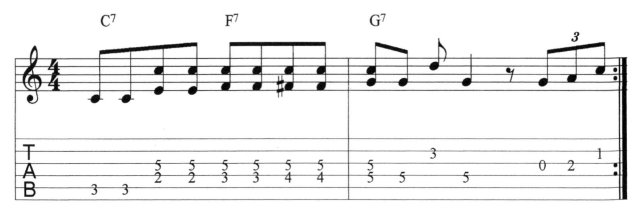

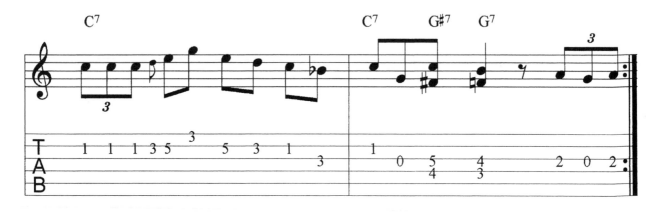

TRUNAROUNDS IN G

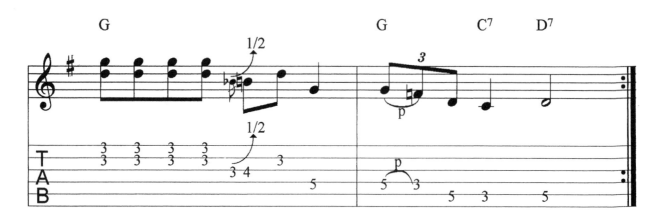

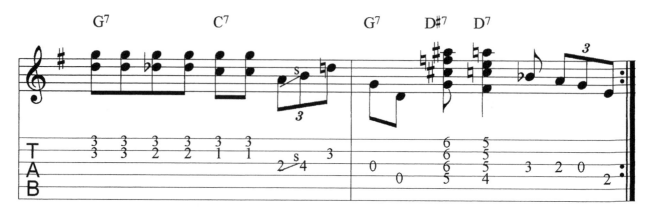

SOMETHING TO THINK ABOUT

Mastering Scale Tones

The three blues chords that harmonize the scale surround each 'box' position. When playing a riff it is important to emphasize chord tones in order to pull a riff through a chord change. Example: When the chord change moves from the I chord to the IV chord (in this example *G7 to C7*), alter the previous riff to include a *C7* chord tone. When playing through the I-IV change *G7* to *D7*, we have two chord shapes to fool around with – one behind the box and one in front of the box. **Something to think about!**

We have placed these examples at the 8th fret – the key of *G*. We do this to accommodate acoustic players, and to give you the opportunity to play blues riffs in a different key. Move these examples up three frets and you will be in the key of *A*.

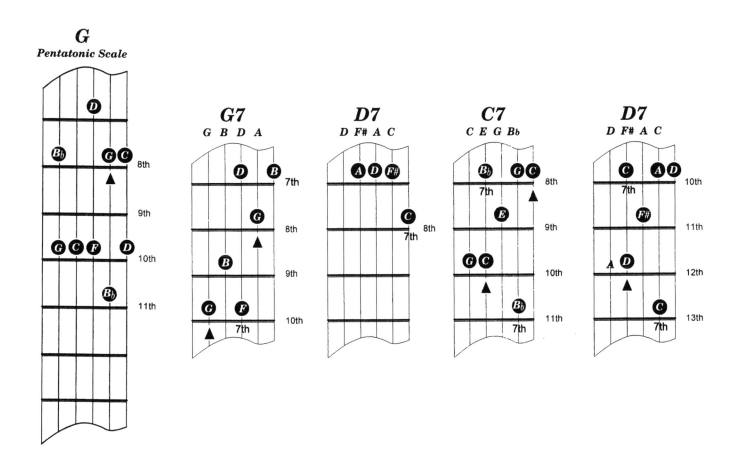

175

12-Bar Blues Arrangement Templates

ARRANGEMENT TEMPLATES

We have explained several technical devices blues musicians use to begin and end a song, and each changes the style of the arrangement. While there are many variations, we now present four of the most common types of beginning and ending patterns.

In the following examples we utilize a musical composition device called "first ending" and "second ending", which encompasses the eleventh and twelfth measures. These two measures are designated by a "bracket" placed over them. The first ending is marked with the number "1" placed at the beginning of measure eleven. Double dots are placed to the left of the double bar line at the end of the twelfth measure, which ends on the V chord, directing you back to the set of double dots placed to the right of the beginning of measure 1. Play through the first ending each time you wish to repeat the arrangement. The second ending marked with the number "2" is the "ending" of the song. The twelfth measure in the second ending, ends on the 1 chord. **Important**: Do not play both endings back-to-back! Play through the first ending to repeat verses. To end the song, skip the first ending and play the second ending.

Each of the 10 jam tracks on the CD uses one of these templates.

BEGINNINGS-TURNAROUNDS-ENDINGS

12-Bar Blues Introduction

It is not uncommon for the band to play through the entire 12-bar chord change before either the vocalist or instrumentalists begin their performance. In this illustration, we begin with pick-up notes leading to the first beat in measure one. The band then plays through the entire 12-bars, including the turnaround which is tagged to the V chord, and leading back to the first measure.

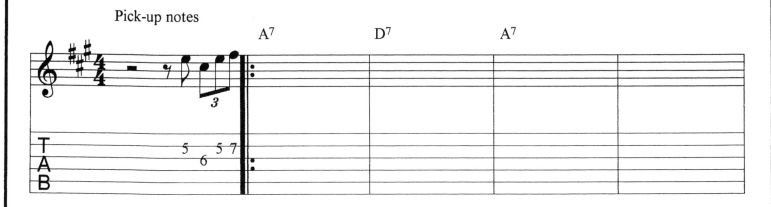

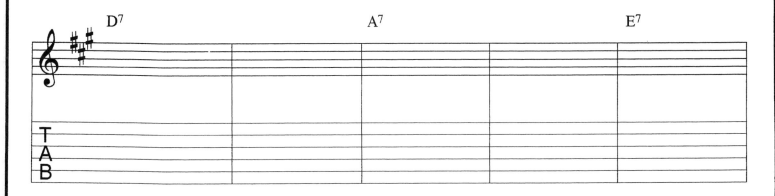

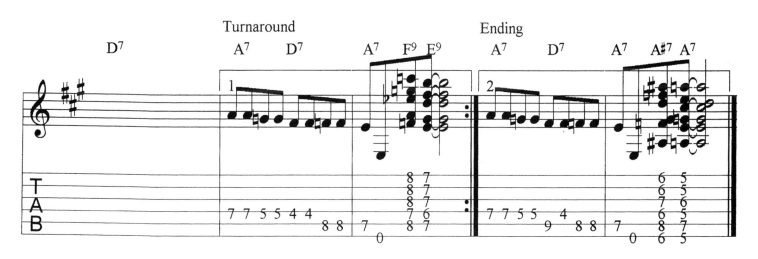

BEGINNINGS-TURNAROUNDS-ENDINGS

Vamp

A **vamp** is a musical device used by musicians to fill *dead time* – that time on stage during a performance when there is a pause between songs. A vamp is simply a rhythm pattern normally played over the I chord, and continues until a cue is given to begin the 12-bar change. A vamp may commence with a group of *pick-up* notes, or a simple *count-off* leading to the I chord.

BEGINNINGS-TURNAROUNDS-ENDINGS

Beginning with the Turnaround

In this illustration, we abbreviate the introduction even further by simply beginning with the turnaround, measures eleven and twelve. Pick-up notes are not required. We begin, in measure eleven on the I chord, and play through measures twelve, tagged with the V chord. The vocalists or instrumentalists comes in on the first measure of the arraignment.

BEGINNINGS-TURNAROUNDS-ENDINGS
From the Five

Another common way of beginning a blues song is to start from the V chord, the ninth measure, and play through the turnaround, tagged with the V chord, and then return to the I chord, first measure of the song. Usually at this point, the vocals come in or the band plays an instrumental verse. In this illustration, we begin by playing pick-up notes that lead into the V chord, ninth measure. We then play through the 12-bar change. Ending 1 is tagged with the V chord, a turnaround. Ending 2 is tagged with the I chord, ending the song.

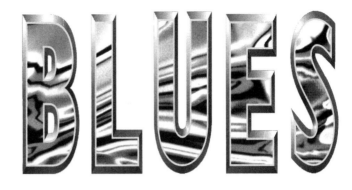

ADVANCED TECHNIQUES

Moving the box – Parallel movement

Mixolydian "B.B. King" scale

Arpeggio movement

Using the capo

Riffs in other keys

ADVANCED TECHNIQUES

Moving the "E" Box Pentatonic Scale

PARALLEL MOVEMENT

While it is possible to improvise over the entire 12-bar blues progression by using one box scale pattern played over the three blues chords, there are other alternatives. Shifting *boxes* is a common device employed to extend our usage of the entire range of the fret board. This shift is called a *parallel movement*, and can be accomplished by changing *key centers*. We may simply play pentatonic scales that follow the chord changes, shifting to a different minor pentatonic scale over each chord. For example, in the key of A, we may play the A minor pentatonic scale over the I chord A, fifth fret; we may play the D minor pentatonic scale over the IV chord D7, tenth fret; and the E minor pentatonic over the V chord E7 at the twelfth fret. (Illustration One). In other words, we can follow the blues changes by playing a minor pentatonic scale whose root matches the tonic note of each chord. You will notice that the fingering pattern for each scale remains the same. In other words, the fingering pattern that creates the A minor pentatonic scale at the fifth fret, will produce the correct notes for the D and E minor pentatonic scales played at their respective frets.

A simple way to look at this parallel box movement is to relate the E form box to the *form one bar chord*. Played at the fifth fret, this chord is an A7 chord. Moved to the tenth fret, the same chord fingering becomes a D7 chord, and moved to the twelfth fret, it becomes an E7 chord.

In the following Illustrations, we present the three minor pentatonic scales and their respective bar chords. As the chords may be moved to follow the blues rhythm pattern, so also, may the pentatonic scale fingering pattern be moved to follow the lead pattern.

ILLUSTRATION ONE
a minor pentatonic

In Illustration One, we present the A minor pentatonic scale played at the fifth fret, and the A7th bar chord also played on the fifth fret.

ILLUSTRATION TWO
D minor pentatonic

The same chord fingering played at the tenth fret create a D7th chord.

ILLUSTRATION THREE
E minor pentatonic

In Illustration Three, we present the same scale fingering pattern played at the twelfth fret. This is now an E minor pentatonic scale.

Moving the *E* Box Pentatonic Scale

ILLUSTRATION ONE

A minor pentatonic scale

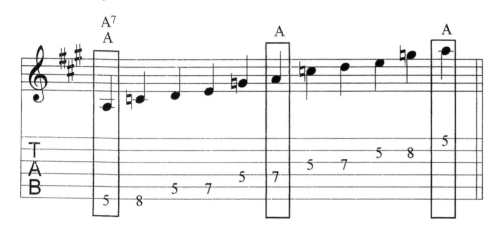

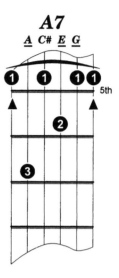

ILLUSTRATION TWO

D minor pentatonic scale

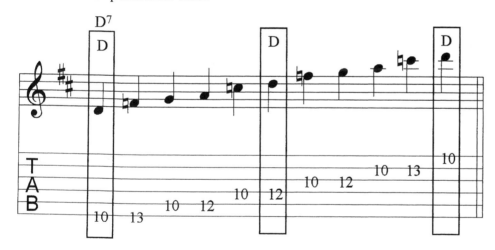

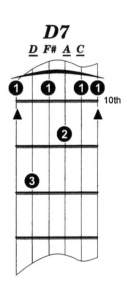

ILLUSTRATION THREE

E minor pentatonic scale

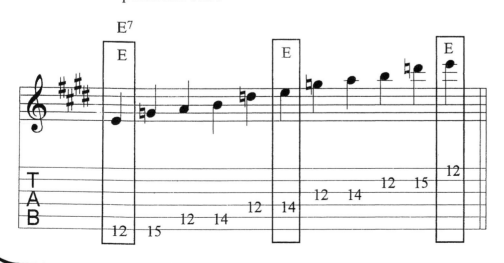

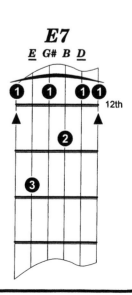

Moving the *E* Box Pentatonic Scale
Parallel Movement Study

As we have demonstrated, it is possible to create a simple riff and continue playing it over and over, the same group of notes and the same position, over each chord in the blues chord progression. This is the simplest way to play the blues. However, moving this same riff (moving the box) to follow the chord changes adds interest to a solo. In Illustration Two, we create a simple riff at the fifth fret and it is played over the I chord *A7*. We move it to the tenth fret to play it over the IV chord *D7-D9*. We then move it to the twelfth fret to play it over the V chord *E-E9*. This is a simplistic concept, but blues players have been using the idea for years! Remember, in blues, the chords are never played simply as major chords. In this exercise, we use the standard *seventh* chord fingering shapes. Remember also that, ninth chords are extensions of the seventh chord (a little theory here).

ILLUSTRATION ONE

In this exercise, the fingering is tricky. But, with a little practice, you will find it is a lick that sounds good and can be used in numerous riffs.

ILLUSTRATION TWO

This is a very common blues lick often used as a turnaround. It will require practice in order to perfect the finger movement, so take your time and keep at it!

ILLUSTRATION THREE

Illustration Three is another *lick* that is played over each of the three chords that are used in a standard blues progression. In this example, the chord progression is I-IV to the V chord.

ADVANCED TECHNIQUES

Moving the Box

ILLUSTRATION ONE

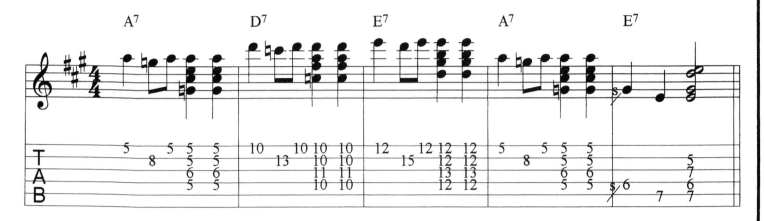

ILLUSTRATION TWO

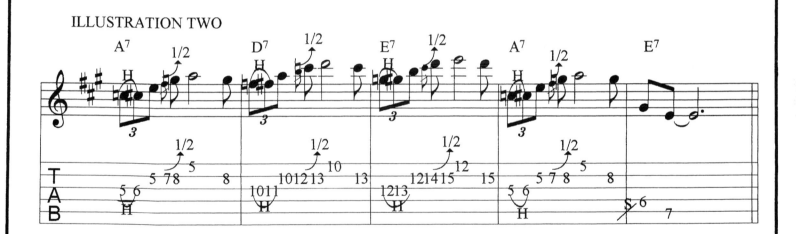

ILLUSTRATION THREE

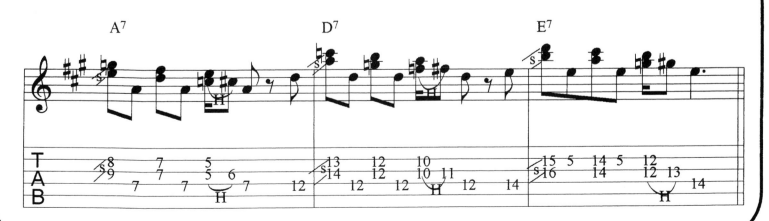

12-Bar Parallel Solo

The 12-Bar Parallel Solo is a further demonstration of how a lick or riff may be developed as a rhythm figure and then played over the blues chord progression. Notice how this riff is a two-bar phrase when played over the I and IV chords. It is necessary to reduce this riff to a one-bar phrase when played over measures nine, ten, eleven and twelve, which are one-bar chord changes. This riff is a great back-up device that works well when played behind a vocal.

In measures nine and ten, the two-bar riff is divided by playing the first bar of the riff in bar nine and the second bar of the riff in bar ten. This process is repeated in measures eleven and twelve.

PLAYING TIP

There's no substitute for experience. Search out good players and get into a jam session with them. Don't be afraid of playing poorly - you become a good player by learning how to overcome mistakes.

12 BAR PARALLEL SOLO

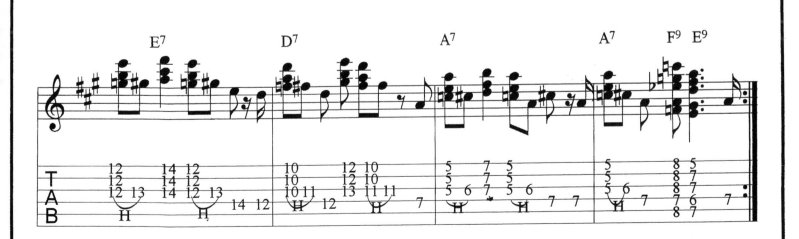

Mixolydian Scale

THE B.B. KING BLUES SCALE

The **Mixolydian scale** is a modal scale played from the fifth note of a diatonic scale, and is called a dominant scale for it contains the flat seventh note that creates the dominant seventh chord of that key. The Mixolydian scale may be thought of as a major scale with a flatted seventh. (The A Mixolydian scale comes from the D major scale – the fifth note of the D sale is the note A. The IV chord in the key of A is D, and in blues, it is played as D7. When we explore the A Mixolydian scale, we find it contains four notes common to the A minor pentatonic scale – notes A, D, E, and G (Illustration One). The A Mixolydian scale has a "major third". Blues guitarist maneuver through this major-third – minor-third complexity by playing "passing tones".

ILLUSTRATION ONE
A MIXOLYDIAN SCALE

In Illustration One, we present the A Mixolydian scale played at the fifth fret. We have placed circles around those notes of the A Mixolydian scale that are common to the A Minor Pentatonic scale.

ILLUSTRATION TWO
NOTES OF THE A7 CHORD

All tones of the A7 chord (A C# E G) are found within the A Mixolydian scale.

ILLUSTRATION THREE
NOTES OF THE D7 CHORD

Three of the four tones that create the D7 chord (D F# A) are found within the A Mixolydian scale. The note C natural – the tone that creates the dominant seventh tone – is not in the scale, and this must always be taken into consideration when playing the A Mixolydian scale over the D7 chord.

ILLUSTRATION FOUR

Three of the four tones that creat the E7 chord (EBD) are found in the A Mixolydian scale. The third of the chord, the note G# is not in the scale, and this must always be taken into consideration when playing the a Mixolydian Scale over the E7 chord.

─── A PERFORMANCE NOTE───

When playing a Mixolydian scale, the chord tones make great "passing tones". Place them in a riff played as eighth or sixteenth notes and you will create a smooth transition between scale tones and chord tones.

MIXOLYDIAN SCALE

ILLUSTRATION ONE

A Mixolydian scale

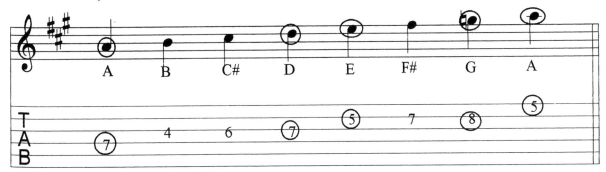

ILLUSTRATION TWO

Notes of the A7 chord in the A Mixolydian scale
A C# E G

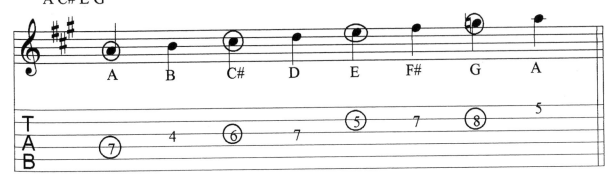

ILLUSTRATION THREE

Notes of the D7 chord in the Mixolydian scale
D F# A

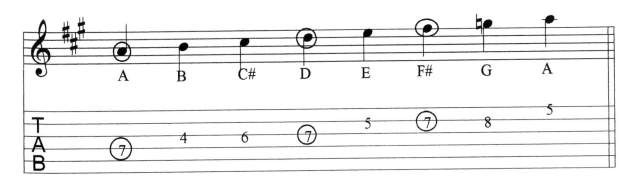

ILLUSTRATION FOUR

Notes of the E7 chord in the A Mixolydian scale
E B D

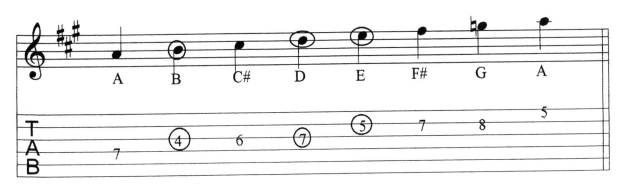

Mixolydian Scale Study Continued

B.B. King's phrasing is deceptively simple. He uses a sparseness of notes; yet, his riffs are surprisingly sophisticated, because he always plays the *right* notes. His unique style of blues comes from his uncanny ability to weave his musical lines in and out of the Blues minor penatonic scale and the Mixolydian major scale. This combination provides a scale that contains the root, second/ninth, fourth, flat third, fourth, fifth, six, and flat seventh. The wealth of blues music created by B.B. King, by utilizing this combination of scales, is a testament to the man's originality and the power that comes from precision string bending. In many ways, the Mixolydian scale, as used in blues phrasing, is a *hybrid* scale. When playing the notes of the *A* Mixolydian scale as shown in Illustration Two, you will notice that they do not necessarily sound musical! As is often the case in blues phrasing, it is *how* the chosen notes are played that makes a riff sizzle. By experimenting with the Mixolydian scale, you will come to realize that it is the *bending* of notes that creates the B.B. King style!

ILLUSTRATION ONE

In Illustration One, we present the A Mixolydian scale played at the tenth fret. It includes those notes of the scale that are most commonly used in riff construction.

ILLUSTRATION TWO

In Illustration Two, we present a B.B. King stylé riff. It begins with a full bend – B to C#, a Mixolydian note not found in the "Blues Scale". The riff ends with a half step bend C to C natural, a note that is found in the pentatonic blues scale. The riff ends on a cut note. Make the bend and then stop the note, terminating the one beat sustain.

ILLUSTRATION THREE

This example incorporates three basic blues expression tools-a slide, a full step bend, and vibrato.

ILLUSTRATION FOUR

This example makes a great opening statement.

THE MIXOLYDIAN SCALE

ILLUSTRATION ONE

A Mixolydian scale - 10th position

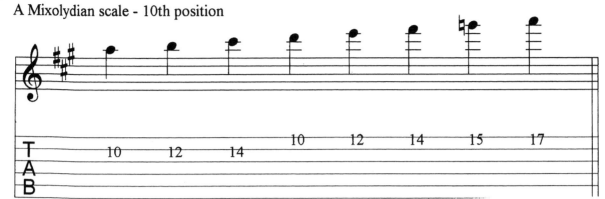

ILLUSTRATION TWO

Mixolydian riff

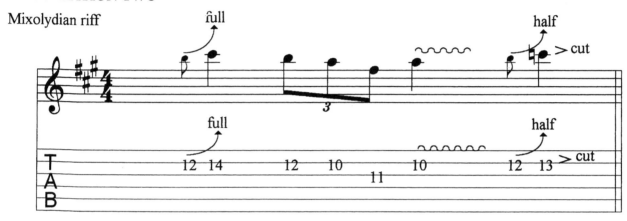

ILLUSTRATION THREE

Mixolydian riff

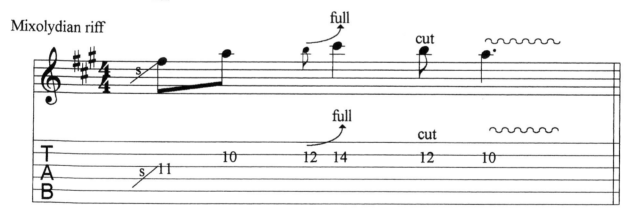

ILLUSTRATION FOUR

Mixolydian riff

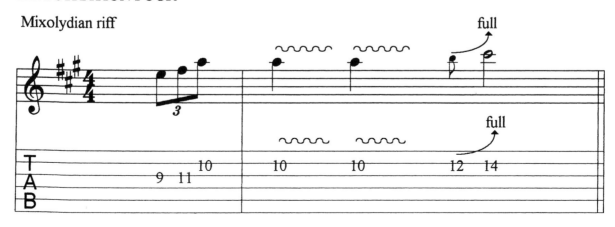

Four Position Riffs

A great blues solo is often comprised of a series of well developed riffs and licks tht are connected in new and interesting ways. On the following page, we present four riffs – each played at a different position, so that we may demonstrate this concept.

ILLUSTRATION ONE

In Illustration One, we create a basic riff idea, first measure, played in the lower octave of the *A* minor pentatonic scale, fifth fret, then expand upon it in the second measure.

ILLUSTRATION TWO

In Illustration Two, we take the same idea and play it within the fifth position *A* pentatonic box and further develop the idea in the second measure. We also incorporate a bend-release.

ILLUSTRATION THREE

In Illustration Three, we move the simple riff idea to the upper octave of the fifth position box scale. In the second measure, we expand upon the idea, adding additional notes and incorporating a half-step bend.

ILLUSTRATION FOUR

In Illustration Four, we stay at the tenth fret and expand upon the original idea by including notes of the *A* Mixolydian scale. In the third measure, we incorporate bent notes which creates the tonal color of the B.B. King style of blues phrasing. Notice how the riff sounds major instead of minor.

EXTENDING THE BOX

ILLUSTRATION ONE
LOWER OCTAVE

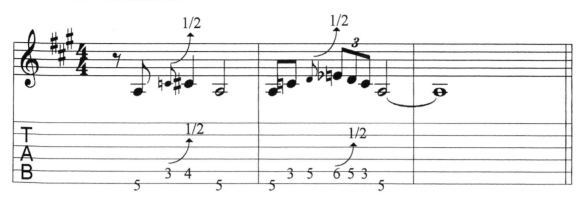

ILLUSTRATION TWO

INSIDE THE BOX

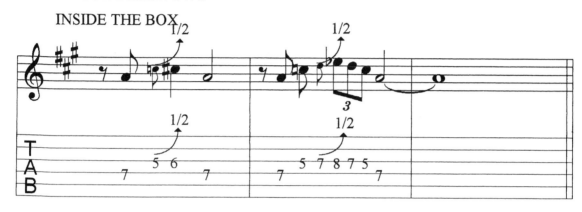

ILLUSTRATION THREE

UPPER OCTAVE

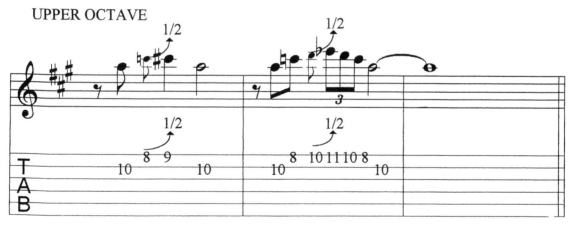

ILLUSTRATION FOUR
FOUR POSITION RIFF

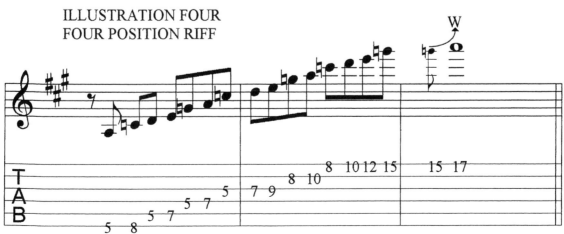

ADVANCED TECHNIQUES

Arpeggio Movement

When the individual tones of a chord are sounded one after another, it is called a *broken chord,* or *arpeggio.* Arpeggios provide the guitarist with a unique way to add variety and new sounds to established licks because arpeggios are bridges between scales and chords. Also, playing across a chord covers the strings more quickly than playing a scale movement. Arpeggios may be played in ascending or descending order.

ILLUSTRATION ONE

In Illustration One (a). We present the barr *D* major (*E* chord form) played at the tenth fret. In Illustration One (b), we present the barr *D* major (*E* chord form), played at the seventh fret.

ILLUSTRATION TWO

Illustration Two, opens with a four note chromatic run, which is a musical device that works well in blues improvisation. The next part of this riff utilizes a B.B. King phrase. The riffs end with a partial barr *D7* arpeggio. The note *C* natural, marked with a circle, is the flat seventh of the *D7* chord. As an experiment, try holding the tenth, eleventh, and twelfth tones down together and allow them to sustain – a great riff idea.

ILLUSTRATION THREE

In Illustration Three, we begin with the *A* minor pentatonic scale, fifth fret box, then move to the *G* chord form played at the seventh fret which creates a *D* chord. We include slides and a bend-release expression tool in the second measure.

ILLUSTRATION FOUR

This exercise is a pure dominant 7th arpeggio. Try reversing each arpeggio. Arpeggios also can be picked in any order. Always be on the lookout for chord arpeggios. The more seventh chord forms you know, the more arpeggios you know.

ILLUSTRATION ONE (a)

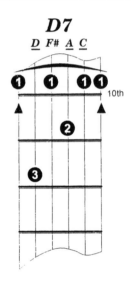

ILLUSTRATION ONE (b)

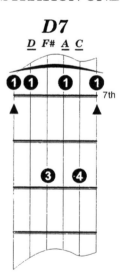

ARPEGGIO MOVEMENT

ILLUSTRATION TWO

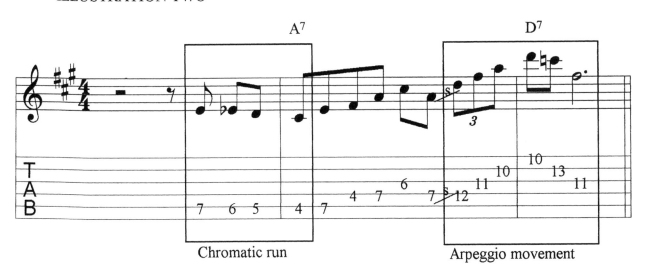

ILLUSTRATION THREE

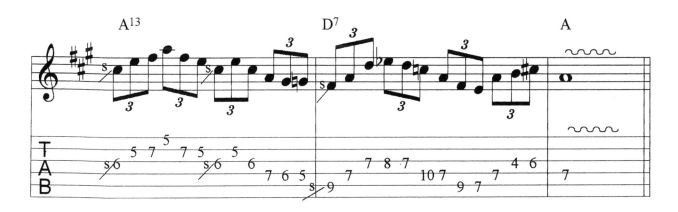

ILLUSTRATION FOUR

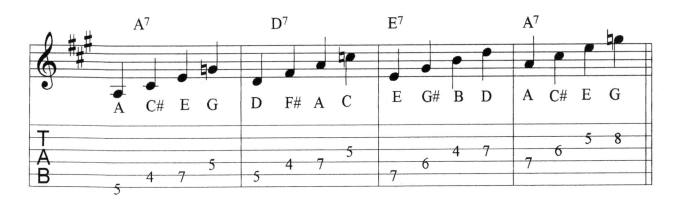

ACCOUSTIC BLUES RIFFS

Courtesy of Anthony Smith

Blues fills licks and tricks

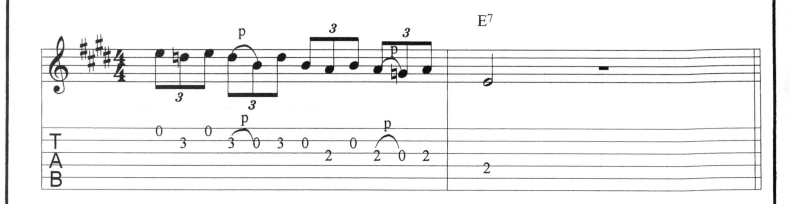

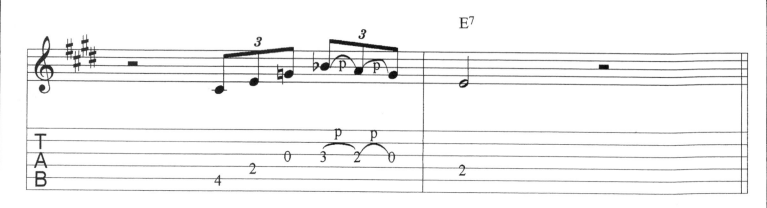

*Use a half-step slide

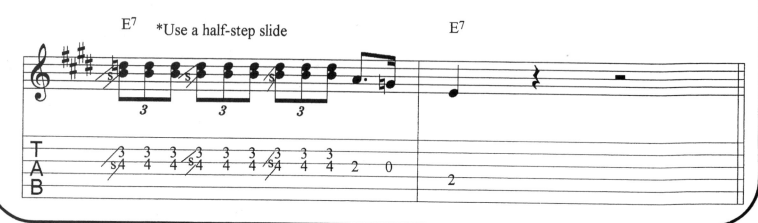

ACCOUSTIC BLUES RIFFS

Courtesy of Anthony Smith

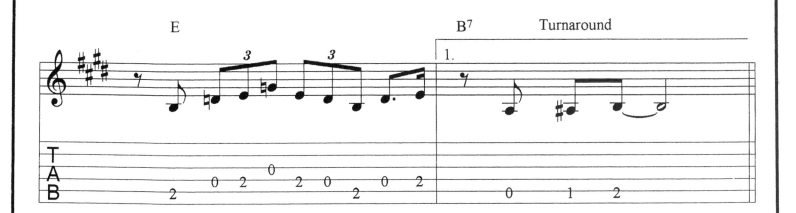

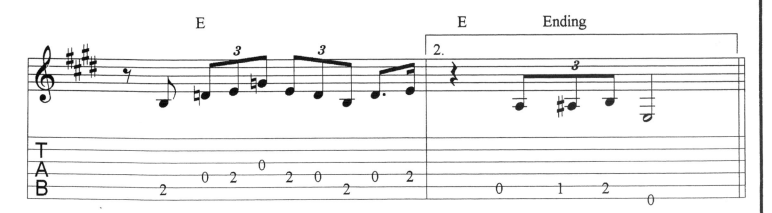

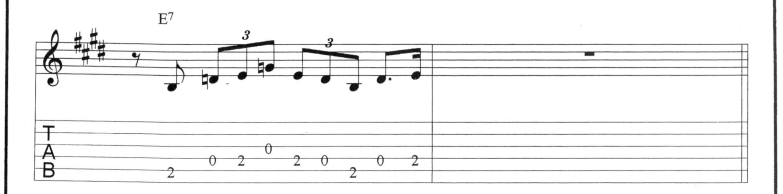

Blues lick in G

ACCOUSTIC BLUES RIFFS
Courtesy of Anthony Smith

Blues lick going to the dominant 7th

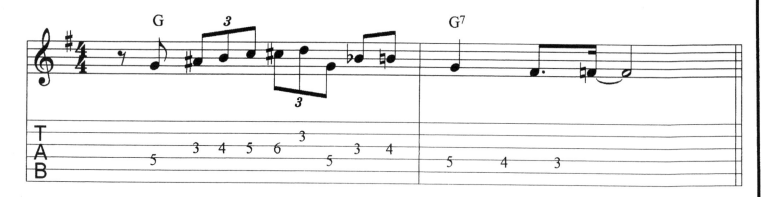

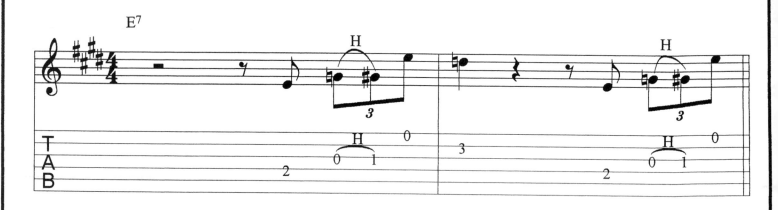

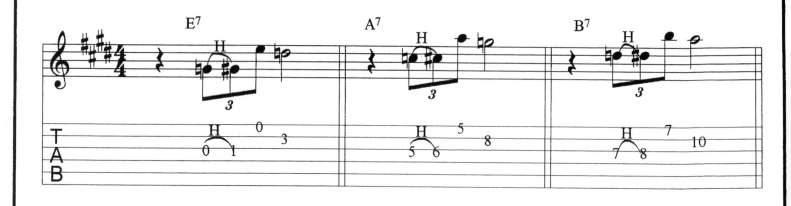

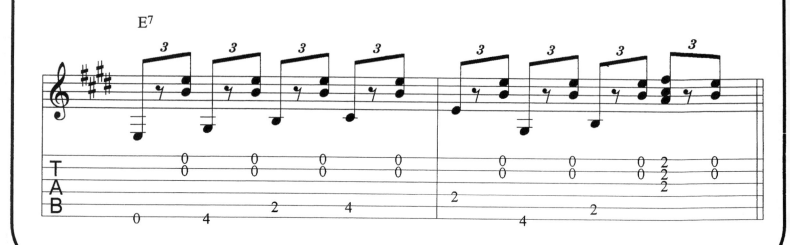

ACCOUSTIC BLUES RIFFS

Courtesy of Anthony Smith

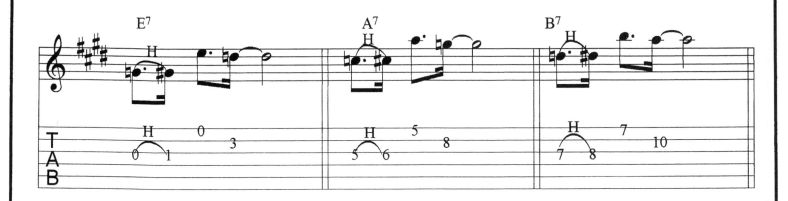

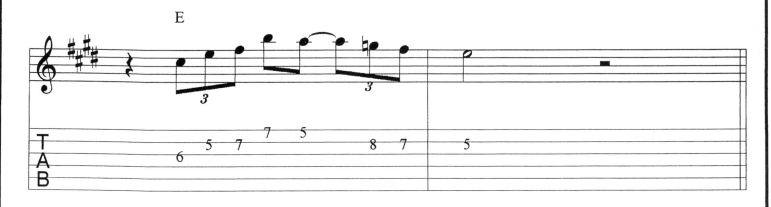

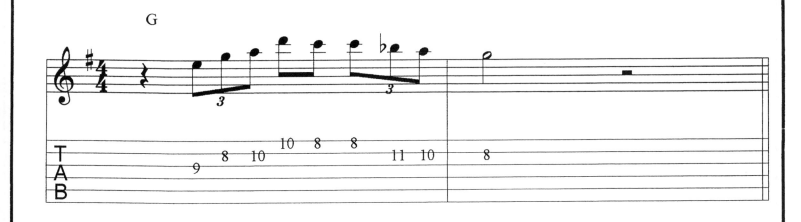

ACCOUSTIC BLUES RIFFS

Courtesy of Anthony Smith

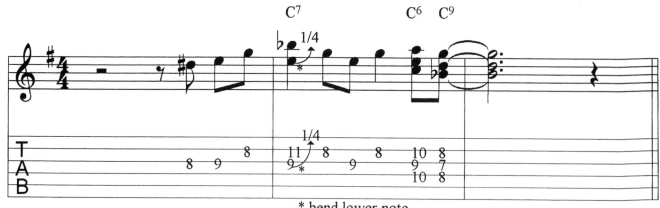

* bend lower note

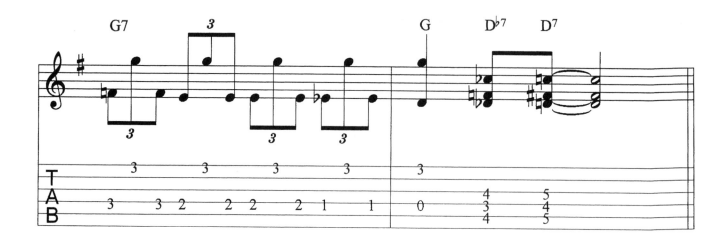

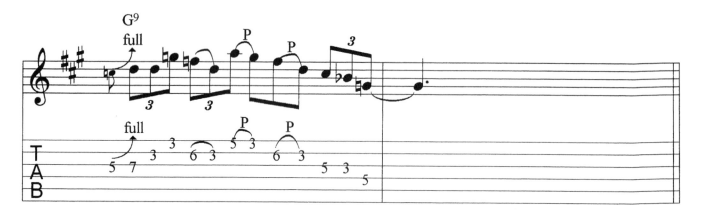

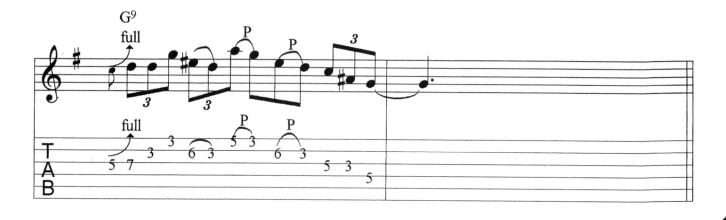